VB.NET AND
COM ODBC

Working with the ADO and ODBC Drivers

Richard Thomas Edwards

CONTENTS

Welcome To ODBC
What is ODBC

THE FIRST THING THAT SHOULD POP OUT AT YOU IS THE FACT THAT THIS ENTIRE BOOK IS DEDICATED TO THE USE OF THE ADODB.RECORDSET USING ODBC DRIVERS. Another book will include the use of DAO AND ODBC

Now, it is time to explore ODBC.

ODBC stands for Open Database Connectivity and it has be a standard for 30 years. Yes, it is true that ADO can be used with providers and can connect to a universe of well-known databases, in can also use ODBC driver related databases such as Oracle and SQL Server.

Which also brings us to another problem. Once the recordset is created, it can be treated as any other recordset and so, my example code – which can't be written any other way will be the same across all books on the subject.

With that said, below is an image of all the drivers:

Name	Type	Data
(Default)	REG_SZ	(value not set)
Microsoft Access Driver (*.mdb)	REG_SZ	Installed
Microsoft dBase Driver (*.dbf)	REG_SZ	Installed
Microsoft Excel Driver (*.xls)	REG_SZ	Installed
Microsoft FoxPro Driver (*.dbf)	REG_SZ	Installed
Microsoft ODBC for Oracle	REG_SZ	Installed
Microsoft Paradox Driver (*.db)	REG_SZ	Installed
Microsoft Text Driver (*.txt; *.csv)	REG_SZ	Installed
Microsoft Visual FoxPro Driver	REG_SZ	Installed
SQL Server	REG_SZ	Installed
SQL Server Native Client 11.0	REG_SZ	Installed

You can use the Microsoft Access Driver for Exporting a supported ISAM format, but you can't do the reverse.

```
Dim cnstr As String = "Driver={Microsoft Access Driver
(*.mdb)};dbq=C:\Program Files (x86)\Microsoft Visual
Studio\VB98\NWIND.MDB;"

Dim strQuery As String = "Select * From [Products.dbf]"

Dim cn As New ADODB.Connection
cn.ConnectionString = cnstr
cn.Open()
cn.Execute("Select * INTO[dBase III;hdr=yes;Database=" &
Application.StartupPath & "\].[products.dbf]from [products];")
```

This works fine but when I try to do the reverse, no matter how I try to write it:

```
Dim cn As New ADODB.Connection
cn.ConnectionString = "Driver={Microsoft Access Driver
(*.mdb)};dBase III;hdr=yes;dbq=" & Application.StartupPath & "\;"
cn.Open()
```

Operation has been canceled.

On the other hand, this works:

```
Dim cn As New ADODB.Connection
cn.ConnectionString = "Driver={Microsoft dBase Driver
(*.dbf)};dbq=" & Application.StartupPath & "\;"
```

```
cn.Open()

Dim rs As New ADODB.Recordset
rs.let_ActiveConnection(cn)
rs.CursorLocation = CursorLocationEnum.adUseClient
rs.LockType = LockTypeEnum.adLockOptimistic
rs.Open(strQuery)

Debug.Print(rs.RecordCount)
Debug.Print(rs.Fields.Count)
```

ADODB Objects
Connection, Command, and Recordset

The code below is designed to provide you with what I know works on my machine. You may have to modify it to work on yours.

```
Dim cnstr As String = "Driver={Microsoft Access Driver
(*.mdb)};dbq=C:\Program Files (x86)\Microsoft Visual
Studio\VB98\NWIND.MDB;"

Dim strQuery As String = "Select * From Products"
```

Connection, Command and Recordset

```
Dim cn As New ADODB.Connection
cn.Open(cnstr)

Dim cmd As New ADODB.Command
cmd.let_ActiveConnection(cn)
cmd.CommandType = CommandTypeEnum.adCmdText
cmd.CommandText = "Select * From Products"
cmd.Execute()

Dim rs As New ADODB.Recordset
rs.CursorLocation = CursorLocationEnum.adUseClient
rs.LockType = LockTypeEnum.adLockOptimistic
rs.Open(cmd)
```

Connection and Recordset

```
Dim cn As New ADODB.Connection
cn.Open(cnstr)

Dim rs As New ADODB.Recordset
rs.let_ActiveConnection(cn)
rs.CursorLocation = CursorLocationEnum.adUseClient
rs.LockType = LockTypeEnum.adLockOptimistic
rs.Open(strQuery)
```

Command and Recordset

```
Dim cmd As New ADODB.Command
cmd.let_ActiveConnection(cnstr)
cmd.CommandType = CommandTypeEnum.adCmdText
cmd.CommandText = "Select * From Products"
cmd.Execute()

Dim rs As New ADODB.Recordset
rs.CursorLocation = CursorLocationEnum.adUseClient
rs.LockType = LockTypeEnum.adLockOptimistic
rs.Open(cmd)
```

Recordset

```
Dim rs As New ADODB.Recordset
rs.let_ActiveConnection(cnstr)
rs.CursorLocation = CursorLocationEnum.adUseClient
rs.LockType = LockTypeEnum.adLockOptimistic
rs.Open(strQuery)
```

Working with the Recordset
The OleDb sidekick

The recordset works perfectly fine for what we want to accomplish. For most of the code in this book, the following routines get the job done.

```
For x = 0 to rs.Fields.Count-1
    Something needs the field name
Next
Rs.MoveFirst()
For x = 0 to rs.Fields.Count-1
    Something needs the field Value
Next
```

Or:

```
Rs.MoveFirst()
For y = 0 To rs.RecordCount -1
    For x = 0 to rs.Fields.Count -1
        Something needs the field Name, the Field Value, field Name
    Next
    Rs.MoveNext
Next
```

Or:

```
Rs.MoveFirst()
For x = 0 to rs.Fields.Count -1
```

Something needs the field name
Something needs the field Value
Next

Or:

For x = 0 to rs.Fields.Count-1
    Something needs the field name
    Rs.MoveFirst()
    For y = 0 To rs.RecordCount -1
        Something needs the field Value
    Next
    Rs.MoveNext
Next

The first two are for horizontal views, the second two for vertical views. But there comes a time when you want to bind directly to things like the DataGridView with the normal way first and then I'll show you how it can be used in the unbound mode.

Okay, so you have a recordset filled with the information you want to bind to the DataGridView1.DataSource.

```
Dim rs As New ADODB.Recordset
rs.let_ActiveConnection(cnstr)
rs.CursorLocation = CursorLocationEnum.adUseClient
rs.LockType = LockTypeEnum.adLockOptimistic
rs.Open(strQuery)
```

Using the DataTable

```
Dim dt As New DataTable
Dim da As New OleDb.OleDbDataAdapter
da.Fill(dt, rs)
dt.TableName = "Products"
```

```
DataGridView1.DataSource = dt
```

Using the DataSet

```
Dim ds As New DataSet
ds.Tables.Add(dt)

DataGridView1.DataSource = ds.Tables(0)
```

Using the DataView

```
Dim dv As DataView = dt.DefaultView
DataGridView1.DataSource = dv
```

And all three examples produce the same view:

ProductID	ProductName	SupplierID	CategoryID	QuantityPerUnit	UnitPrice	UnitsInStock	UnitsOnOrde ^
1	Chai	1	1	10 boxes x 20 bags	18	39	0
2	Chang	1	1	24 - 12 oz bottles	19	17	40
3	Aniseed Syrup	1	2	12 - 550 ml bottles	10	13	70
4	Chef Anton's Caj...	2	2	48 - 6 oz jars	22	53	0
5	Chef Anton's Gu...	2	2	36 boxes	21.35	0	0
6	Grandma's Boyse...	3	2	12 - 8 oz jars	25	120	0
7	Uncle Bob's Orga...	3	7	12 - 1 lb pkgs.	30	15	0
8	Northwoods Cran...	3	2	12 - 12 oz jars	40	6	0
9	Mishi Kobe Niku	4	6	18 - 500 g pkgs.	97	29	0
10	Ikura	4	8	12 - 200 ml jars	31	31	0
11	Queso Cabrales	5	4	1 kg pkg.	21	22	30
12	Queso Mancheg...	5	4	10 - 500 g pkgs.	38	86	0
13	Konbu	6	8	2 kg box	6	24	0
14	Tofu	6	7	40 - 100 g pkgs.	23.25	35	0
15	Genen Shouyu	6	2	24 - 250 ml bottles	15.5	39	0
16	Pavlova	7	3	32 - 500 g boxes	17.45	29	0
17	Alice Mutton	7	6	20 - 1 kg tins	39	0	0
18	Carnarvon Tigers	7	8	16 kg pkg.	62.5	42	0
19	Teatime Chocolat...	8	3	10 boxes x 12 pie...	9.2	25	0
20	Sir Rodney's Mar...	8	3	30 gift boxes	81	40	0

But what is really making this work the OleDbDataAdapter or the DataSet, DataTable or DataView?

As it turns out, the OleDbDataAdapter performs the heavy lifting and populates the DataTable does, exactly, same way the manual version does

```
Dim cnstr As String = "Driver={Microsoft Access Driver
(*.mdb)};dbq=C:\Program Files (x86)\Microsoft Visual
Studio\VB98\NWIND.MDB;"

Dim strQuery As String = "Select * From Products"

Dim rs As New ADODB.Recordset
rs.let_ActiveConnection(cnstr)
rs.CursorLocation = CursorLocationEnum.adUseClient
rs.LockType = LockTypeEnum.adLockOptimistic
rs.Open(strQuery)
```

Horizontal view using the DataTable

```
For x As Integer = 0 To rs.Fields.Count - 1
    dt.Columns.Add(rs.Fields(x).Name)
Next

For y As Integer = 0 To rs.RecordCount - 1
    Dim dr As System.Data.DataRow = dt.NewRow
    For x As Integer = 0 To rs.Fields.Count - 1
        dr.Item(rs.Fields(x).Name) = rs.Fields(x).Value
    Next
    dt.Rows.Add(dr)
    rs.MoveNext()
Next

DataGridView1.DataSource = dt
```

Horizontal view using the DataSet

```
Dim ds As New DataSet
ds.Tables.Add(dt)

DataGridView1.DataSource = ds.Tables(0)
```

Horizontal view using the DataView

```
Dim dv As DataView = dt.DefaultView
DataGridView1.DataSource = dv
```

Vertical view using the DataTable

```
dt.Columns.Add("Property Name")
For y As Integer = 0 To rs.RecordCount - 1
    dt.Columns.Add("Rows" & y)
Next
For x As Integer = 0 To rs.Fields.Count - 1
    Dim dr As System.Data.DataRow = dt.NewRow
    dr.Item("Property Name") = rs.Fields(x).Name
    rs.MoveFirst()

    For y As Integer = 0 To rs.RecordCount - 1
        dr.Item("Rows" & y) = rs.Fields(x).Value
```

```
            rs.MoveNext()
        Next
        dt.Rows.Add(dr)
    Next

    DataGridView1.DataSource = dt
```

Vertical view using the DataSet

```
    Dim ds As New DataSet
    ds.Tables.Add(dt)

    DataGridView1.DataSource = ds.Tables(0)
```

Vertical view using the DataView

```
    Dim dv As DataView = dt.DefaultView
    DataGridView1.DataSource = dv
```

This code produces this view:

Property Name	Rows0	Rows1	Rows2	Rows3
ProductID	1	2	3	4
ProductName	Chai	Chang	Aniseed Syrup	Chef Anton's Caj...
SupplierID	1	1	1	2
CategoryID	1	1	2	2
QuantityPerUnit	10 boxes x 20 bags	24 - 12 oz bottles	12 - 550 ml bottles	48 - 6 oz jars
UnitPrice	18	19	10	22
UnitsInStock	39	17	13	53
UnitsOnOrder	0	40	70	0
ReorderLevel	10	25	25	0
Discontinued	False	False	False	False

How to build your code

The code presented in this book is designed to be pieced together with the ADODB Objects code placed at the top of the routine you've chosen to use with it.

Of course, you can write it anyway you want to. I just designed the code this way to shorten the number of pages needed to complete this book. Shorten the number of pages, not shorten you on the amount of coding examples.

ASP

B ELOW ARE EXAMPLES OF ODBC USING AN ODBC DRIVER WITH ASP.

```
Dim ws As Object = CreateObject("WScript.Shell")
Dim fso As Object = CreateObject("Scripting.FileSystemObject")
Dim txtstream as Object = fso.OpenTextFile(ws.CurrentDirectory +
"\Products.asp", 2, True, -2)
```

Horizontal Reports

```
txtstream.WriteLine("<hmtl>")
txtstream.WriteLine("<head>")
txtstream.WriteLine("<title>Products</title>")
txtstream.WriteLine("<style type='text/css'>")
txtstream.WriteLine("th")
txtstream.WriteLine("{")
txtstream.WriteLine("   COLOR: darkred;")
txtstream.WriteLine("   BACKGROUND-COLOR: #eeeeee;")
txtstream.WriteLine("   FONT-FAMILY:font-family: Cambria, serif;")
```

```
txtstream.WriteLine("   FONT-SIZE: 12px;")
txtstream.WriteLine("   text-align: left;")
txtstream.WriteLine("   white-Space: nowrap='nowrap';")
txtstream.WriteLine("}")
txtstream.WriteLine("td")
txtstream.WriteLine("{")
txtstream.WriteLine("   COLOR: navy;")
txtstream.WriteLine("   BACKGROUND-COLOR: #eeeeee;")
txtstream.WriteLine("   FONT-FAMILY: font-family: Cambria, serif;")
txtstream.WriteLine("   FONT-SIZE: 12px;")
txtstream.WriteLine("   text-align: left;")
txtstream.WriteLine("   white-Space: nowrap='nowrap';")
txtstream.WriteLine("}")
txtstream.WriteLine("</style>")

txtstream.WriteLine("</head>")
txtstream.WriteLine("<body>")
txtstream.WriteLine("<center>")
txtstream.WriteLine("</br>")
txtstream.WriteLine("<table border=0 cellspacing=3 cellpadding=3>")
txtstream.WriteLine("<%")
txtstream.WriteLine("Response.Write(""""<tr>"""" & vbcrlf)")
For x = 0 To Rs.Fields.Count-1
txtstream.WriteLine("Response.Write(""""<th align='left' nowrap='nowrap'>" &
rs.Fields(x).Name & "</th>"""" & vbcrlf)")
    Next
txtstream.WriteLine("Response.Write(""""</tr>"""" & vbcrlf)")
rs.MoveFirst()
Do While rs.EOF = false
    txtstream.WriteLine("Response.Write(""""<tr>"""" & vbcrlf)")
    For x = 0 To Rs.Fields.Count-1
    txtstream.WriteLine("Response.Write(""""<td                    align='left'
nowrap='nowrap'>" & rs.Fields(x).Value & "</td>"""" & vbcrlf)")
```

```
            Next
            txtstream.WriteLine("Response.Write(""</tr>""" & vbcrlf)")
            rs.MoveNext()
        Next
        txtstream.WriteLine("%>")
        txtstream.WriteLine("</table>")
        txtstream.WriteLine("</body>")
        txtstream.WriteLine("</html>")
        txtstream.Close()
```

Vertical Reports

```
        Dim ws As Object  = CreateObject("WScript.Shell")
        Dim fso As Object  = CreateObject("Scripting.FileSystemObject")
        Dim  txtstream  as  Object      =  fso.OpenTextFile(ws.CurrentDirectory  +
"\Products.asp", 2, True, -2)
        txtstream.WriteLine("<hmtl>")
        txtstream.WriteLine("<head>")
        txtstream.WriteLine("<title>Products</title>")
        txtstream.WriteLine("<style type='text/css'>")
        txtstream.WriteLine("th")
        txtstream.WriteLine("{")
        txtstream.WriteLine("    COLOR: darkred;")
        txtstream.WriteLine("    BACKGROUND-COLOR: #eeeeee;")
        txtstream.WriteLine("    FONT-FAMILY:font-family: Cambria, serif;")
        txtstream.WriteLine("    FONT-SIZE: 12px;")
        txtstream.WriteLine("    text-align: left;")
        txtstream.WriteLine("    white-Space: nowrap='nowrap';")
        txtstream.WriteLine("}")
        txtstream.WriteLine("td")
        txtstream.WriteLine("{")
        txtstream.WriteLine("    COLOR: navy;")
        txtstream.WriteLine("    BACKGROUND-COLOR: #eeeeee;")
```

```
txtstream.WriteLine("   FONT-FAMILY: font-family: Cambria, serif;")
txtstream.WriteLine("   FONT-SIZE: 12px;")
txtstream.WriteLine("   text-align: left;")
txtstream.WriteLine("   white-Space: nowrap='nowrap';")
txtstream.WriteLine("}")
txtstream.WriteLine("</style>")

txtstream.WriteLine("</head>")
txtstream.WriteLine("<body>")
txtstream.WriteLine("<center>")
txtstream.WriteLine("</br>")
txtstream.WriteLine("<table border=0 cellspacing=3 cellpadding=3>")
txtstream.WriteLine("<%")
For x = 0 To Rs.Fields.Count-1
    txtstream.WriteLine("Response.Write(""<tr><th           align='left'
nowrap='nowrap'>" & rs.Fields(x).Name & "</th>"" & vbcrlf)")
    rs.MoveFirst()
    Do While rs.EOF = false
    txtstream.WriteLine("Response.Write(""<td                align='left'
nowrap='true'><input    type=text    value="""    &    rs.Fields(x).Value    &
"""></input></td>"" & vbcrlf)")
        rs.MoveNext()
    Loop
    txtstream.WriteLine("Response.Write(""</tr>"" & vbcrlf)")
Next
txtstream.WriteLine("%>")
txtstream.WriteLine("</table>")
txtstream.WriteLine("</body>")
txtstream.WriteLine("</html>")
txtstream.Close()
```

Horizontal Tables

```
Dim ws As Object  = CreateObject("WScript.Shell")
Dim fso As Object  = CreateObject("Scripting.FileSystemObject")
Dim  txtstream  as  Object  =  fso.OpenTextFile(ws.CurrentDirectory  +
"\Products.asp", 2, True, -2)
txtstream.WriteLine("<hmtl>")
txtstream.WriteLine("<head>")
txtstream.WriteLine("<title>Products</title>")
txtstream.WriteLine("<style type='text/css'>")
txtstream.WriteLine("th")
txtstream.WriteLine("{")
txtstream.WriteLine("   COLOR: darkred;")
txtstream.WriteLine("   BACKGROUND-COLOR: #eeeeee;")
txtstream.WriteLine("   FONT-FAMILY:font-family: Cambria, serif;")
txtstream.WriteLine("   FONT-SIZE: 12px;")
txtstream.WriteLine("   text-align: left;")
txtstream.WriteLine("   white-Space: nowrap='nowrap';")
txtstream.WriteLine("}")
txtstream.WriteLine("td")
txtstream.WriteLine("{")
txtstream.WriteLine("   COLOR: navy;")
txtstream.WriteLine("   BACKGROUND-COLOR: #eeeeee;")
txtstream.WriteLine("   FONT-FAMILY: font-family: Cambria, serif;")
txtstream.WriteLine("   FONT-SIZE: 12px;")
txtstream.WriteLine("   text-align: left;")
txtstream.WriteLine("   white-Space: nowrap='nowrap';")
txtstream.WriteLine("}")
txtstream.WriteLine("</style>")

txtstream.WriteLine("</head>")
txtstream.WriteLine("<body>")
txtstream.WriteLine("<center>")
txtstream.WriteLine("<%")
For x = 0 To Rs.Fields.Count-1
```

```
        txtstream.WriteLine("Response.Write(""<tr><th                    align='left'
nowrap='nowrap'>" & rs.Fields(x).Name & "</th>""" & vbcrlf)")
        rs.MoveFirst()
        Do While rs.EOF = false
        txtstream.WriteLine("Response.Write(""<td                         align='left'
nowrap='true'><input      type=text     value=""""       &      rs.Fields(x).Value      &
""""></input></td>""" & vbcrlf)")
        rs.MoveNext()
        Loop
        txtstream.WriteLine("Response.Write(""</tr>""" & vbcrlf)")
    Next
    txtstream.WriteLine("%>")
    txtstream.WriteLine("</table>")
    txtstream.WriteLine("</body>")
    txtstream.WriteLine("</html>")
    txtstream.Close()
```

Vertical Tables

```
    Dim cnstr as String = Driver={Microsoft Access Driver (*.mdb)}; DBQ
=C:\Program Files (x86)\Microsoft Visual Studio\VB98\NWIND.MDB"
    Dim strQuery as String = "Select * From [Products]"

    Dim ws As Object  = CreateObject("WScript.Shell")
    Dim fso As Object  = CreateObject("Scripting.FileSystemObject")
    Dim   txtstream   as   Object      =   fso.OpenTextFile(ws.CurrentDirectory   +
"\Products.asp", 2, True, -2)
    txtstream.WriteLine("<hmtl>")
    txtstream.WriteLine("<head>")
    txtstream.WriteLine("<title>Products</title>")
    txtstream.WriteLine("<style type='text/css'>")
    txtstream.WriteLine("th")
    txtstream.WriteLine("{")
```

```
txtstream.WriteLine("    COLOR: darkred;")
txtstream.WriteLine("    BACKGROUND-COLOR: #eeeeee;")
txtstream.WriteLine("    FONT-FAMILY:font-family: Cambria, serif;")
txtstream.WriteLine("    FONT-SIZE: 12px;")
txtstream.WriteLine("    text-align: left;")
txtstream.WriteLine("    white-Space: nowrap='nowrap';")
txtstream.WriteLine("}")
txtstream.WriteLine("td")
txtstream.WriteLine("{")
txtstream.WriteLine("    COLOR: navy;")
txtstream.WriteLine("    BACKGROUND-COLOR: #eeeeee;")
txtstream.WriteLine("    FONT-FAMILY: font-family: Cambria, serif;")
txtstream.WriteLine("    FONT-SIZE: 12px;")
txtstream.WriteLine("    text-align: left;")
txtstream.WriteLine("    white-Space: nowrap='nowrap';")
txtstream.WriteLine("}")
txtstream.WriteLine("</style>")

txtstream.WriteLine("</head>")
txtstream.WriteLine("<body>")
txtstream.WriteLine("<center>")
txtstream.WriteLine("</br>")
txtstream.WriteLine("</br>")
txtstream.WriteLine("<%")
For x = o To Rs.Fields.Count-1
    txtstream.WriteLine("Response.Write(""<tr><th                align='left'
nowrap='nowrap'>" & rs.Fields(x).Name & "</th>""" & vbcrlf)")
        rs.MoveFirst()
        Do While rs.EOF = false
        txtstream.WriteLine("Response.Write(""<td                align='left'
nowrap='true'><input        type=text       value=""""" &        rs.Fields(x).Value        &
""""""></input></td>""" & vbcrlf)")
        rs.MoveNext()
```

```
        Loop
        txtstream.WriteLine("Response.Write("""</tr>""" & vbcrlf)")
Next
txtstream.WriteLine("%>")
txtstream.WriteLine("</table>")
txtstream.WriteLine("</body>")
txtstream.WriteLine("</html>")
txtstream.Close()
```

ASPX Examples

B ELOW ARE EXAMPLES OF ODBC USING AN ODBC DRIVER WITH ASPX.

```
Dim ws As Object  = CreateObject("WScript.Shell")
Dim fso As Object  = CreateObject("Scripting.FileSystemObject")
Dim  txtstream  as  Object  =  fso.OpenTextFile(ws.CurrentDirectory  +
"\Products.aspx", 2, True, -2)
```

Horizontal Reports

```
txtstream.WriteLine("<hmtl>")
txtstream.WriteLine("<head>")
txtstream.WriteLine("<title>Products</title>")
txtstream.WriteLine("<style type='text/css'>")
txtstream.WriteLine("th")
txtstream.WriteLine("{")
txtstream.WriteLine("   COLOR: darkred;")
txtstream.WriteLine("   BACKGROUND-COLOR: #eeeeee;")
txtstream.WriteLine("   FONT-FAMILY:font-family: Cambria, serif;")
txtstream.WriteLine("   FONT-SIZE: 12px;")
txtstream.WriteLine("   text-align: left;")
```

```
txtstream.WriteLine("    white-Space: nowrap='nowrap';")
txtstream.WriteLine("}")
txtstream.WriteLine("td")
txtstream.WriteLine("{")
txtstream.WriteLine("    COLOR: navy;")
txtstream.WriteLine("    BACKGROUND-COLOR: #eeeeee;")
txtstream.WriteLine("    FONT-FAMILY: font-family: Cambria, serif;")
txtstream.WriteLine("    FONT-SIZE: 12px;")
txtstream.WriteLine("    text-align: left;")
txtstream.WriteLine("    white-Space: nowrap='nowrap';")
txtstream.WriteLine("}")
txtstream.WriteLine("</style>")
txtstream.WriteLine("</head>")
txtstream.WriteLine("<body>")
txtstream.WriteLine("<center>")
txtstream.WriteLine("</br>")
txtstream.WriteLine("<table border=0 cellspacing=3 cellpadding=3>")
txtstream.WriteLine("<%")
txtstream.WriteLine("Response.Write("""<tr>""" & vbcrlf)")
For x = 0 To Rs.Fields.Count-1
txtstream.WriteLine("Response.Write("""<th align='left' nowrap='nowrap'>" &
rs.Fields(x).Name & "</th>""" & vbcrlf)")
Next
txtstream.WriteLine("Response.Write("""</tr>""" & vbcrlf)")
rs.MoveFirst()
Do While rs.EOF = false
    txtstream.WriteLine("Response.Write("""<tr>""" & vbcrlf)")
    For x = 0 To Rs.Fields.Count-1
    txtstream.WriteLine("Response.Write("""<td                align='left'
nowrap='nowrap'>" & rs.Fields(x).Value & "</td>""" & vbcrlf)")
    Next
    txtstream.WriteLine("Response.Write("""</tr>""" & vbcrlf)")
    rs.MoveNext()
```

```
Next
txtstream.WriteLine("%>")
txtstream.WriteLine("</table>")
txtstream.WriteLine("</body>")
txtstream.WriteLine("</html>")
txtstream.Close()
```

Vertical Reports

```
txtstream.WriteLine("<hmtl>")
txtstream.WriteLine("<head>")
txtstream.WriteLine("<title>Products</title>")
txtstream.WriteLine("<style type='text/css'>")
txtstream.WriteLine("th")
txtstream.WriteLine("{")
txtstream.WriteLine("   COLOR: darkred;")
txtstream.WriteLine("   BACKGROUND-COLOR: #eeeeee;")
txtstream.WriteLine("   FONT-FAMILY:font-family: Cambria, serif;")
txtstream.WriteLine("   FONT-SIZE: 12px;")
txtstream.WriteLine("   text-align: left;")
txtstream.WriteLine("   white-Space: nowrap='nowrap';")
txtstream.WriteLine("}")
txtstream.WriteLine("td")
txtstream.WriteLine("{")
txtstream.WriteLine("   COLOR: navy;")
txtstream.WriteLine("   BACKGROUND-COLOR: #eeeeee;")
txtstream.WriteLine("   FONT-FAMILY: font-family: Cambria, serif;")
txtstream.WriteLine("   FONT-SIZE: 12px;")
txtstream.WriteLine("   text-align: left;")
txtstream.WriteLine("   white-Space: nowrap='nowrap';")
txtstream.WriteLine("}")
txtstream.WriteLine("</style>")
```

```
txtstream.WriteLine("</head>")
txtstream.WriteLine("<body>")
txtstream.WriteLine("<center>")
txtstream.WriteLine("</br>")
txtstream.WriteLine("<table border=0 cellspacing=3 cellpadding=3>")
txtstream.WriteLine("<%")
For x = 0 To Rs.Fields.Count-1
    txtstream.WriteLine("Response.Write(""<tr><th                align='left'
nowrap='nowrap'>" & rs.Fields(x).Name & "</th>"" & vbcrlf)")
    rs.MoveFirst()
    Do While rs.EOF = false
    txtstream.WriteLine("Response.Write(""<td                align='left'
nowrap='true'><input    type=text    value="""    &    rs.Fields(x).Value    &
"""></input></td>"" & vbcrlf)")
    rs.MoveNext()
    Loop
    txtstream.WriteLine("Response.Write(""</tr>"" & vbcrlf)")
Next
txtstream.WriteLine("%>")
txtstream.WriteLine("</table>")
txtstream.WriteLine("</body>")
txtstream.WriteLine("</html>")
txtstream.Close()
```

Horizontal Tables

```
txtstream.WriteLine("<hmtl>")
txtstream.WriteLine("<head>")
txtstream.WriteLine("<title>Products</title>")
txtstream.WriteLine("<style type='text/css'>")
txtstream.WriteLine("th")
txtstream.WriteLine("{")
txtstream.WriteLine("    COLOR: darkred;")
```

```vb
txtstream.WriteLine("   BACKGROUND-COLOR: #eeeeee;")
txtstream.WriteLine("   FONT-FAMILY:font-family: Cambria, serif;")
txtstream.WriteLine("   FONT-SIZE: 12px;")
txtstream.WriteLine("   text-align: left;")
txtstream.WriteLine("   white-Space: nowrap='nowrap';")
txtstream.WriteLine("}")
txtstream.WriteLine("td")
txtstream.WriteLine("{")
txtstream.WriteLine("   COLOR: navy;")
txtstream.WriteLine("   BACKGROUND-COLOR: #eeeeee;")
txtstream.WriteLine("   FONT-FAMILY: font-family: Cambria, serif;")
txtstream.WriteLine("   FONT-SIZE: 12px;")
txtstream.WriteLine("   text-align: left;")
txtstream.WriteLine("   white-Space: nowrap='nowrap';")
txtstream.WriteLine("}")
txtstream.WriteLine("</style>")

txtstream.WriteLine("</head>")
txtstream.WriteLine("<body>")
txtstream.WriteLine("<center>")
txtstream.WriteLine("<%")
For x = 0 To Rs.Fields.Count-1
    txtstream.WriteLine("Response.Write(""<tr><th          align='left' nowrap='nowrap'>" & rs.Fields(x).Name & "</th>""" & vbcrlf)")
    rs.MoveFirst()
    Do While rs.EOF = false
    txtstream.WriteLine("Response.Write(""<td          align='left' nowrap='true'><input    type=text    value="""" & rs.Fields(x).Value & """""></input></td>""" & vbcrlf)")
    rs.MoveNext()
    Loop
    txtstream.WriteLine("Response.Write(""</tr>""" & vbcrlf)")
Next
```

```
txtstream.WriteLine("%>")
txtstream.WriteLine("</table>")
txtstream.WriteLine("</body>")
txtstream.WriteLine("</html>")
txtstream.Close()
```

Vertical Tables

```
txtstream.WriteLine("<hmtl>")
txtstream.WriteLine("<head>")
txtstream.WriteLine("<title>Products</title>")
txtstream.WriteLine("<style type='text/css'>")
txtstream.WriteLine("th")
txtstream.WriteLine("{")
txtstream.WriteLine("    COLOR: darkred;")
txtstream.WriteLine("    BACKGROUND-COLOR: #eeeeee;")
txtstream.WriteLine("    FONT-FAMILY:font-family: Cambria, serif;")
txtstream.WriteLine("    FONT-SIZE: 12px;")
txtstream.WriteLine("    text-align: left;")
txtstream.WriteLine("    white-Space: nowrap='nowrap';")
txtstream.WriteLine("}")
txtstream.WriteLine("td")
txtstream.WriteLine("{")
txtstream.WriteLine("    COLOR: navy;")
txtstream.WriteLine("    BACKGROUND-COLOR: #eeeeee;")
txtstream.WriteLine("    FONT-FAMILY: font-family: Cambria, serif;")
txtstream.WriteLine("    FONT-SIZE: 12px;")
txtstream.WriteLine("    text-align: left;")
txtstream.WriteLine("    white-Space: nowrap='nowrap';")
txtstream.WriteLine("}")
txtstream.WriteLine("</style>")

txtstream.WriteLine("</head>")
```

```
        txtstream.WriteLine("<body>")
        txtstream.WriteLine("<center>")
        txtstream.WriteLine("</br>")
        txtstream.WriteLine("</br>")
        txtstream.WriteLine("<%")
        For x = 0 To Rs.Fields.Count-1
            txtstream.WriteLine("Response.Write(""<tr><th                align='left'
nowrap='nowrap'>" & rs.Fields(x).Name & "</th>""" & vbcrlf)")
            rs.MoveFirst()
            Do While rs.EOF = false
            txtstream.WriteLine("Response.Write(""<td                     align='left'
nowrap='true'><input    type=text    value=""""    &    rs.Fields(x).Value    &
""""></input></td>""" & vbcrlf)")
            rs.MoveNext()
            Loop
            txtstream.WriteLine("Response.Write(""</tr>""" & vbcrlf)")
        Next
        txtstream.WriteLine("%>")
        txtstream.WriteLine("</table>")
        txtstream.WriteLine("</body>")
        txtstream.WriteLine("</html>")
        txtstream.Close()
```

HTA Examples

BELOW ARE EXAMPLES OF ADO USING ODBC AND CREATING HTA FILES.

```
Dim ws As Object  = CreateObject("WScript.Shell")
Dim fso As Object  = CreateObject("Scripting.FileSystemObject")
Dim  txtstream  as  Object  =  fso.OpenTextFile(ws.CurrentDirectory  +
"\Products.hta", 2, True, -2)
```

Horizontal Reports

```
txtstream.WriteLine("<hmtl>")
txtstream.WriteLine("<head>")
txtstream.WriteLine("<HTA:APPLICATION ")
txtstream.WriteLine("ID = 'Products' ")
txtstream.WriteLine("APPLICATIONNAME = 'Products' ")
txtstream.WriteLine("SCROLL = 'yes' ")
txtstream.WriteLine("SINGLEINSTANCE = 'yes' ")
txtstream.WriteLine("WINDOWSTATE = 'maximize' >")
txtstream.WriteLine("<title>Products</title>")
txtstream.WriteLine("<style type='text/css'>")
txtstream.WriteLine("th")
```

```
txtstream.WriteLine("{")
txtstream.WriteLine("    COLOR: darkred;")
txtstream.WriteLine("    BACKGROUND-COLOR: #eeeeee;")
txtstream.WriteLine("    FONT-FAMILY:font-family: Cambria, serif;")
txtstream.WriteLine("    FONT-SIZE: 12px;")
txtstream.WriteLine("    text-align: left;")
txtstream.WriteLine("    white-Space: nowrap='nowrap';")
txtstream.WriteLine("}")
txtstream.WriteLine("td")
txtstream.WriteLine("{")
txtstream.WriteLine("    COLOR: navy;")
txtstream.WriteLine("    BACKGROUND-COLOR: #eeeeee;")
txtstream.WriteLine("    FONT-FAMILY: font-family: Cambria, serif;")
txtstream.WriteLine("    FONT-SIZE: 12px;")
txtstream.WriteLine("    text-align: left;")
txtstream.WriteLine("    white-Space: nowrap='nowrap';")
txtstream.WriteLine("}")
txtstream.WriteLine("</style>")
txtstream.WriteLine("</head>")
txtstream.WriteLine("<body>")
txtstream.WriteLine("<center>")
txtstream.WriteLine("</br>")
txtstream.WriteLine("<table border=0 cellspacing=3 cellpadding=3>")

txtstream.WriteLine("<tr>")
For x = 0 To Rs.Fields.Count-1
txtstream.WriteLine("<th align='left' nowrap='nowrap'>" & rs.Fields(x).Name
& "</th>")
Next
txtstream.WriteLine("</tr>")
rs.MoveFirst()
Do While rs.EOF = false
    txtstream.WriteLine("<tr>")
```

```
      For x = 0 To Rs.Fields.Count-1
        txtstream.WriteLine("<td          align='left'      nowrap='nowrap'>"      &
rs.Fields(x).Value & "</td>")
      Next
      txtstream.WriteLine("</tr>")
      rs.MoveNext()
    Next

    txtstream.WriteLine("</table>")
    txtstream.WriteLine("</body>")
    txtstream.WriteLine("</html>")
    txtstream.Close()
```

Vertical Reports

```
    txtstream.WriteLine("<hmtl>")
    txtstream.WriteLine("<head>")
    txtstream.WriteLine("<HTA:APPLICATION ")
    txtstream.WriteLine("ID = 'Products' ")
    txtstream.WriteLine("APPLICATIONNAME = 'Products' ")
    txtstream.WriteLine("SCROLL = 'yes' ")
    txtstream.WriteLine("SINGLEINSTANCE = 'yes' ")
    txtstream.WriteLine("WINDOWSTATE = 'maximize' >")
    txtstream.WriteLine("<title>Products</title>")
    txtstream.WriteLine("<style type='text/css'>")
    txtstream.WriteLine("th")
    txtstream.WriteLine("{")
    txtstream.WriteLine("   COLOR: darkred;")
    txtstream.WriteLine("   BACKGROUND-COLOR: #eeeeee;")
    txtstream.WriteLine("   FONT-FAMILY:font-family: Cambria, serif;")
    txtstream.WriteLine("   FONT-SIZE: 12px;")
    txtstream.WriteLine("   text-align: left;")
    txtstream.WriteLine("   white-Space: nowrap='nowrap';")
```

```
txtstream.WriteLine("}")
txtstream.WriteLine("td")
txtstream.WriteLine("{")
txtstream.WriteLine("    COLOR: navy;")
txtstream.WriteLine("    BACKGROUND-COLOR: #eeeeee;")
txtstream.WriteLine("    FONT-FAMILY: font-family: Cambria, serif;")
txtstream.WriteLine("    FONT-SIZE: 12px;")
txtstream.WriteLine("    text-align: left;")
txtstream.WriteLine("    white-Space: nowrap='nowrap';")
txtstream.WriteLine("}")
txtstream.WriteLine("</style>")

txtstream.WriteLine("</head>")
txtstream.WriteLine("<body>")
txtstream.WriteLine("<center>")
txtstream.WriteLine("</br>")
txtstream.WriteLine("<table border=0 cellspacing=3 cellpadding=3>")

For x = 0 To Rs.Fields.Count-1
    txtstream.WriteLine("<tr><th    align='left'    nowrap='nowrap'>"    &
rs.Fields(x).Name & "</th>")
    rs.MoveFirst()
    Do While rs.EOF = false
    txtstream.WriteLine("<td    align='left'  nowrap='true'><input  type=text
value=""" & rs.Fields(x).Value & """></input></td>")
    rs.MoveNext()
    Loop
    txtstream.WriteLine("</tr>")
Next

txtstream.WriteLine("</table>")
txtstream.WriteLine("</body>")
txtstream.WriteLine("</html>")
```

txtstream.Close()

```
txtstream.WriteLine("<hmtl>")
txtstream.WriteLine("<head>")
txtstream.WriteLine("<HTA:APPLICATION ")
txtstream.WriteLine("ID = 'Products' ")
txtstream.WriteLine("APPLICATIONNAME = 'Products' ")
txtstream.WriteLine("SCROLL = 'yes' ")
txtstream.WriteLine("SINGLEINSTANCE = 'yes' ")
txtstream.WriteLine("WINDOWSTATE = 'maximize' >")
txtstream.WriteLine("<title>Products</title>")
txtstream.WriteLine("<style type='text/css'>")
txtstream.WriteLine("th")
txtstream.WriteLine("{")
txtstream.WriteLine("    COLOR: darkred;")
txtstream.WriteLine("    BACKGROUND-COLOR: #eeeeee;")
txtstream.WriteLine("    FONT-FAMILY:font-family: Cambria, serif;")
txtstream.WriteLine("    FONT-SIZE: 12px;")
txtstream.WriteLine("    text-align: left;")
txtstream.WriteLine("    white-Space: nowrap='nowrap';")
txtstream.WriteLine("}")
txtstream.WriteLine("td")
txtstream.WriteLine("{")
txtstream.WriteLine("    COLOR: navy;")
txtstream.WriteLine("    BACKGROUND-COLOR: #eeeeee;")
txtstream.WriteLine("    FONT-FAMILY: font-family: Cambria, serif;")
txtstream.WriteLine("    FONT-SIZE: 12px;")
txtstream.WriteLine("    text-align: left;")
txtstream.WriteLine("    white-Space: nowrap='nowrap';")
txtstream.WriteLine("}")
txtstream.WriteLine("</style>")
```

```
txtstream.WriteLine("</head>")
txtstream.WriteLine("<body>")
txtstream.WriteLine("<center>")

For x = o To Rs.Fields.Count-1
    txtstream.WriteLine("<tr><th    align='left'    nowrap='nowrap'>"    &
rs.Fields(x).Name & "</th>")
        rs.MoveFirst()
        Do While rs.EOF = false
        txtstream.WriteLine("<td    align='left'  nowrap='true'><input  type=text
value="""" & rs.Fields(x).Value & """"></input></td>")
        rs.MoveNext()
        Loop
        txtstream.WriteLine("</tr>")
    Next

txtstream.WriteLine("</table>")
txtstream.WriteLine("</body>")
txtstream.WriteLine("</html>")
txtstream.Close()
```

Vertical Tables

```
txtstream.WriteLine("<hmtl>")
txtstream.WriteLine("<head>")
txtstream.WriteLine("<HTA:APPLICATION ")
txtstream.WriteLine("ID = 'Products' ")
txtstream.WriteLine("APPLICATIONNAME = 'Products' ")
txtstream.WriteLine("SCROLL = 'yes' ")
txtstream.WriteLine("SINGLEINSTANCE = 'yes' ")
txtstream.WriteLine("WINDOWSTATE = 'maximize' >")
txtstream.WriteLine("<title>Products</title>")
```

```
txtstream.WriteLine("<style type='text/css'>")
txtstream.WriteLine("th")
txtstream.WriteLine("{")
txtstream.WriteLine("   COLOR: darkred;")
txtstream.WriteLine("   BACKGROUND-COLOR: #eeeeee;")
txtstream.WriteLine("   FONT-FAMILY:font-family: Cambria, serif;")
txtstream.WriteLine("   FONT-SIZE: 12px;")
txtstream.WriteLine("   text-align: left;")
txtstream.WriteLine("   white-Space: nowrap='nowrap';")
txtstream.WriteLine("}")
txtstream.WriteLine("td")
txtstream.WriteLine("{")
txtstream.WriteLine("   COLOR: navy;")
txtstream.WriteLine("   BACKGROUND-COLOR: #eeeeee;")
txtstream.WriteLine("   FONT-FAMILY: font-family: Cambria, serif;")
txtstream.WriteLine("   FONT-SIZE: 12px;")
txtstream.WriteLine("   text-align: left;")
txtstream.WriteLine("   white-Space: nowrap='nowrap';")
txtstream.WriteLine("}")
txtstream.WriteLine("</style>")

txtstream.WriteLine("</head>")
txtstream.WriteLine("<body>")
txtstream.WriteLine("<center>")
txtstream.WriteLine("</br>")
txtstream.WriteLine("</br>")

For x = 0 To Rs.Fields.Count-1
    txtstream.WriteLine("<tr><th    align='left'    nowrap='nowrap'>"    &
rs.Fields(x).Name & "</th>")
    rs.MoveFirst()
    Do While rs.EOF = false
```

```
        txtstream.WriteLine("<td      align='left'  nowrap='true'><input  type=text
value=""" & rs.Fields(x).Value & """></input></td>")
        rs.MoveNext()
        Loop
        txtstream.WriteLine("</tr>")
    Next

    txtstream.WriteLine("</table>")
    txtstream.WriteLine("</body>")
    txtstream.WriteLine("</html>")
    txtstream.Close()
```

HTML Examples

BELOW ARE EXAMPLES OF ADO USING ODBC AND CREATING HTML.

```
Dim ws As Object  = CreateObject("WScript.Shell")
Dim fso As Object  = CreateObject("Scripting.FileSystemObject")
Dim  txtstream  as  Object  =  fso.OpenTextFile(ws.CurrentDirectory  +
"\Products.html", 2, True, -2)
```

Horizontal Reports

```
txtstream.WriteLine("<hmtl>")
txtstream.WriteLine("<head>")
txtstream.WriteLine("<title>Products</title>")
txtstream.WriteLine("<style type='text/css'>")
txtstream.WriteLine("th")
txtstream.WriteLine("{")
txtstream.WriteLine("   COLOR: darkred;")
txtstream.WriteLine("   BACKGROUND-COLOR: #eeeeee;")
txtstream.WriteLine("   FONT-FAMILY:font-family: Cambria, serif;")
txtstream.WriteLine("   FONT-SIZE: 12px;")
txtstream.WriteLine("   text-align: left;")
```

```
txtstream.WriteLine("   white-Space: nowrap='nowrap';")
txtstream.WriteLine("}")
txtstream.WriteLine("td")
txtstream.WriteLine("{")
txtstream.WriteLine("   COLOR: navy;")
txtstream.WriteLine("   BACKGROUND-COLOR: #eeeeee;")
txtstream.WriteLine("   FONT-FAMILY: font-family: Cambria, serif;")
txtstream.WriteLine("   FONT-SIZE: 12px;")
txtstream.WriteLine("   text-align: left;")
txtstream.WriteLine("   white-Space: nowrap='nowrap';")
txtstream.WriteLine("}")
txtstream.WriteLine("</style>")
txtstream.WriteLine("</head>")
txtstream.WriteLine("<body>")
txtstream.WriteLine("<center>")
txtstream.WriteLine("</br>")
txtstream.WriteLine("<table border=0 cellspacing=3 cellpadding=3>")

txtstream.WriteLine("<tr>")
For x = 0 To Rs.Fields.Count-1
txtstream.WriteLine("<th align='left' nowrap='nowrap'>" & rs.Fields(x).Name
& "</th>")
Next
txtstream.WriteLine("</tr>")
rs.MoveFirst()
Do While rs.EOF = false
    txtstream.WriteLine("<tr>")
    For x = 0 To Rs.Fields.Count-1
    txtstream.WriteLine("<td         align='left'    nowrap='nowrap'>"    &
rs.Fields(x).Value & "</td>")
    Next
    txtstream.WriteLine("</tr>")
    rs.MoveNext()
```

Next

```
txtstream.WriteLine("</table>")
txtstream.WriteLine("</body>")
txtstream.WriteLine("</html>")
txtstream.Close()
```

Vertical Reports

```
txtstream.WriteLine("<hmtl>")
txtstream.WriteLine("<head>")
txtstream.WriteLine("<title>Products</title>")
txtstream.WriteLine("<style type='text/css'>")
txtstream.WriteLine("th")
txtstream.WriteLine("{")
txtstream.WriteLine("   COLOR: darkred;")
txtstream.WriteLine("   BACKGROUND-COLOR: #eeeeee;")
txtstream.WriteLine("   FONT-FAMILY:font-family: Cambria, serif;")
txtstream.WriteLine("   FONT-SIZE: 12px;")
txtstream.WriteLine("   text-align: left;")
txtstream.WriteLine("   white-Space: nowrap='nowrap';")
txtstream.WriteLine("}")
txtstream.WriteLine("td")
txtstream.WriteLine("{")
txtstream.WriteLine("   COLOR: navy;")
txtstream.WriteLine("   BACKGROUND-COLOR: #eeeeee;")
txtstream.WriteLine("   FONT-FAMILY: font-family: Cambria, serif;")
txtstream.WriteLine("   FONT-SIZE: 12px;")
txtstream.WriteLine("   text-align: left;")
txtstream.WriteLine("   white-Space: nowrap='nowrap';")
txtstream.WriteLine("}")
txtstream.WriteLine("</style>")
```

```
txtstream.WriteLine("</head>")
txtstream.WriteLine("<body>")
txtstream.WriteLine("<center>")
txtstream.WriteLine("</br>")
txtstream.WriteLine("<table border=0 cellspacing=3 cellpadding=3>")

For x = 0 To Rs.Fields.Count-1
    txtstream.WriteLine("<tr><th      align='left'      nowrap='nowrap'>"      &
rs.Fields(x).Name & "</th>")
        rs.MoveFirst()
        Do While rs.EOF = false
        txtstream.WriteLine("<td      align='left' nowrap='true'><input   type=text
value="""" & rs.Fields(x).Value & """"></input></td>")
        rs.MoveNext()
        Loop
        txtstream.WriteLine("</tr>")
    Next

txtstream.WriteLine("</table>")
txtstream.WriteLine("</body>")
txtstream.WriteLine("</html>")
txtstream.Close()
```

Horizontal Tables

```
txtstream.WriteLine("<hmtl>")
txtstream.WriteLine("<head>")
txtstream.WriteLine("<title>Products</title>")
txtstream.WriteLine("<style type='text/css'>")
txtstream.WriteLine("th")
txtstream.WriteLine("{")
txtstream.WriteLine("   COLOR: darkred;")
txtstream.WriteLine("   BACKGROUND-COLOR: #eeeeee;")
```

```
txtstream.WriteLine("   FONT-FAMILY:font-family: Cambria, serif;")
txtstream.WriteLine("   FONT-SIZE: 12px;")
txtstream.WriteLine("   text-align: left;")
txtstream.WriteLine("   white-Space: nowrap='nowrap';")
txtstream.WriteLine("}")
txtstream.WriteLine("td")
txtstream.WriteLine("{")
txtstream.WriteLine("   COLOR: navy;")
txtstream.WriteLine("   BACKGROUND-COLOR: #eeeeee;")
txtstream.WriteLine("   FONT-FAMILY: font-family: Cambria, serif;")
txtstream.WriteLine("   FONT-SIZE: 12px;")
txtstream.WriteLine("   text-align: left;")
txtstream.WriteLine("   white-Space: nowrap='nowrap';")
txtstream.WriteLine("}")
txtstream.WriteLine("</style>")

txtstream.WriteLine("</head>")
txtstream.WriteLine("<body>")
txtstream.WriteLine("<center>")

For x = 0 To Rs.Fields.Count-1
    txtstream.WriteLine("<tr><th    align='left'    nowrap='nowrap'>"    &
rs.Fields(x).Name & "</th>")
    rs.MoveFirst()
    Do While rs.EOF = false
    txtstream.WriteLine("<td    align='left' nowrap='true'><input type=text
value="""" & rs.Fields(x).Value & """"></input></td>")
    rs.MoveNext()
    Loop
    txtstream.WriteLine("</tr>")
Next

txtstream.WriteLine("</table>")
```

```
txtstream.WriteLine("</body>")
txtstream.WriteLine("</html>")
txtstream.Close()
```

Vertical Tables

```
txtstream.WriteLine("<hmtl>")
txtstream.WriteLine("<head>")
txtstream.WriteLine("<title>Products</title>")
txtstream.WriteLine("<style type='text/css'>")
txtstream.WriteLine("th")
txtstream.WriteLine("{")
txtstream.WriteLine("    COLOR: darkred;")
txtstream.WriteLine("    BACKGROUND-COLOR: #eeeeee;")
txtstream.WriteLine("    FONT-FAMILY:font-family: Cambria, serif;")
txtstream.WriteLine("    FONT-SIZE: 12px;")
txtstream.WriteLine("    text-align: left;")
txtstream.WriteLine("    white-Space: nowrap='nowrap';")
txtstream.WriteLine("}")
txtstream.WriteLine("td")
txtstream.WriteLine("{")
txtstream.WriteLine("    COLOR: navy;")
txtstream.WriteLine("    BACKGROUND-COLOR: #eeeeee;")
txtstream.WriteLine("    FONT-FAMILY: font-family: Cambria, serif;")
txtstream.WriteLine("    FONT-SIZE: 12px;")
txtstream.WriteLine("    text-align: left;")
txtstream.WriteLine("    white-Space: nowrap='nowrap';")
txtstream.WriteLine("}")
txtstream.WriteLine("</style>")

txtstream.WriteLine("</head>")
txtstream.WriteLine("<body>")
txtstream.WriteLine("<center>")
```

```
txtstream.WriteLine("</br>")
txtstream.WriteLine("</br>")

For x = 0 To Rs.Fields.Count-1
    txtstream.WriteLine("<tr><th        align='left'        nowrap='nowrap'>" &
rs.Fields(x).Name & "</th>")
    rs.MoveFirst()
    Do While rs.EOF = false
    txtstream.WriteLine("<td        align='left' nowrap='true'><input   type=text
value=""" & rs.Fields(x).Value & """></input></td>")
    rs.MoveNext()
    Loop
    txtstream.WriteLine("</tr>")
Next

txtstream.WriteLine("</table>")
txtstream.WriteLine("</body>")
txtstream.WriteLine("</html>")
txtstream.Close()
```

Using a CSV file to create an Excel Spreadsheet

B ELOW ARE EXAMPLES OF ADO USING A ODBC AND CREATING AN EXCEL SPREADSHEET.

Horizontal

```
Dim ws As Object  = CreateObject("WScript.Shell")
Dim fso As Object  = CreateObject("Scripting.FileSystemObject")
Dim txtstream  as  Object  =  fso.OpenTextFile(ws.CurrentDirectory  +
"\Products.csv", 2, True, -2)
Dim tstr as string = ""
For x = 0 To Rs.Fields.Count-1
    If (tstr <> "") Then
        tstr = tstr + ","
    End If
    tstr = tstr + rs.fields(x).Name
Next
txtstream.Writeline(tstr)
```

```
tstr = ""
rs.MoveFirst()
For y as Integer = 0 to rs.RecordCount-1
    For x = 0 To Rs.Fields.Count-1
        If (tstr <> "") Then
            tstr = tstr + ","
        End If
        tstr = tstr & chr(34) & rs.Fields(x).Value & chr(34)
    Next
    txtstream.Writeline(tstr)
    tstr = ""
    rs.MoveNext()
Next
txtstream.Close
ws.Run(ws.CurrentDirectory + "\Products.csv")
```

Vertical


```
Dim ws As Object  = CreateObject("WScript.Shell")
Dim fso As Object  = CreateObject("Scripting.FileSystemObject")
Dim txtstream   as   Object    = fso.OpenTextFile(ws.CurrentDirectory +
"\Products.csv", 2, True, -2)
Dim tstr as string = ""
For x = 0 To Rs.Fields.Count-1
    tstr = rs.fields(x).Name
    rs.MoveFirst()
    For y as Integer = 0 to rs.RecordCount-1
        If (tstr <> "") Then
            tstr = tstr + ","
        End If
        tstr = tstr & chr(34) & rs.Fields(x).Value & chr(34)
```

```
            rs.MoveNext()
        Next
        txtstream.Writeline(tstr)
        tstr = ""
Next
txtstream.Close
ws.Run(ws.CurrentDirectory + "\Products.csv")
```

Creating an Excel Spreadsheet through automation

BELOW IS THE CODE NEEDED TO CREATE AN EXCEL SPREADSHEET USING ADO WITH AN EXCEL DRIVER.

The Horizontal View

```
Dim oExcel As Object  = CreateObject("Excel.Application")
oExcel.Visible = true
Dim wb As Object  = oExcel.Workbooks.Add()
Dim ws As Object  = wb.WorkSheets(1)
ws.Name = "Products"
x=1
y=2
For z = 0 To rs.Fields.Count - 1
   ws.Cells.Item(1, x) = rs.Fields(z).Name
   x=x+1
Next
```

```
x=1
rs.MoveFirst()
Do While rs.EOF = False
  For z = 0 To rs.Fields.Count - 1
    ws.Cells.Item(y, x) = rs.Fields(z).Value
    x=x+1
  Next
  x=1
  y=y+1
  rs.MoveNext
Loop

ws.Columns.HorizontalAlignment = -4131
iret = ws.Columns.AutoFit()
```

The Vertical View

```
Dim oExcel As Object  = CreateObject("Excel.Application")
oExcel.Visible = true
Dim wb As Object  = oExcel.Workbooks.Add()
Dim ws As Object  = wb.WorkSheets(1)
ws.Name = "Products"
x=1
y=2
For z = 0 To rs.Fields.Count - 1
  ws.Cells.Item(x, 1) = rs.Fields(z).Name
  x=x+1
Next
x=1
rs.MoveFirst()
Do While rs.EOF = False
  For z = 0 To rs.Fields.Count - 1
    ws.Cells.Item(x, yx) = rs.Fields(z).Value
```

```
        x=x+1
    Next
    x=1
    y=y+1
    rs.MoveNext
Loop

ws.Columns.HorizontalAlignment = -4131
iret = ws.Columns.AutoFit()
```

Creating a physical Excel Spreadsheet

BELOW IS THE CODE NEEDED TO CREATE A PHYSICAL EXCEL SPREADSHEET USING ADO WITH AN EXCEL DRIVER.

```
Dim ws As Object = createObject("WScript.Shell")
Dim cdir As String = ws.CurrentDirectory + "\Products.xml"
Dim fso As Object = CreateObject("Scripting.FileSystemObject")
Dim txtstream As Object = fso.OpenTextFile(cdir, 2, true, -2)
```

Horizontal

```
txtstream.WriteLine("<?xml version=""1.0""?>")
txtstream.WriteLine("<?mso-application progid=""Excel.Sheet""?>")
txtstream.WriteLine("<Workbook          xmlns=""urn:schemas-microsoft-
com:office:spreadsheet""    xmlns:o=""urn:schemas-microsoft-com:office:office""
xmlns:x=""urn:schemas-microsoft-com:office:excel""    xmlns:ss=""urn:schemas-
```

```
microsoft-com:office:spreadsheet""        xmlns:html=""http://www.w3.org/TR/REC-
html40"">")
        txtstream.WriteLine("      <ExcelWorkbook  xmlns=""urn:schemas-microsoft-
com:office:excel"">")
        txtstream.WriteLine("              <WindowHeight>11835</WindowHeight>")
        txtstream.WriteLine("              <WindowWidth>18960</WindowWidth>")
        txtstream.WriteLine("              <WindowTopX>120</WindowTopX>")
        txtstream.WriteLine("              <WindowTopY>135</WindowTopY>")
        txtstream.WriteLine("              <ProtectStructure>False</ProtectStructure>")
        txtstream.WriteLine("              <ProtectWindows>False</ProtectWindows>")
        txtstream.WriteLine("  </ExcelWorkbook>")
        txtstream.WriteLine("  <Styles>")
        txtstream.WriteLine("                  <Style ss:ID=""s62"">")
        txtstream.WriteLine("                      <Borders/>")
        txtstream.WriteLine("                      <Font
ss:FontName=""Calibri""        x:Family=""Swiss""        ss:Size=""11""
ss:Color=""#000000"" ss:Bold=""1""/>")
        txtstream.WriteLine("                  </Style>")
        txtstream.WriteLine("                  <Style ss:ID=""s63"">")
        txtstream.WriteLine("                      <Alignment
ss:Horizontal=""Left"" ss:Vertical=""Bottom"" ss:Indent=""2""/>")
        txtstream.WriteLine("                      <Font
ss:FontName=""Verdana""        x:Family=""Swiss""        ss:Size=""7.7""
ss:Color=""#000000""/>")
        txtstream.WriteLine("                  </Style>")
        txtstream.WriteLine("  </Styles>")
        txtstream.WriteLine("  <Worksheet ss:Name=""Win32_NetworkAdapter"">")
        txtstream.WriteLine("      <Table  x:FullColumns=""1""   x:FullRows=""1""
ss:DefaultRowHeight=""24.9375"">")
        txtstream.WriteLine("      <Column ss:AutoFitWidth=""1""  ss:Width=""82.5""
ss:Span=""5""/>")
        txtstream.WriteLine("      <Row ss:AutoFitHeight=""0"">")
        For x as integer = 0 to rs.Fields.Count-1
```

```
txtstream.WriteLine("                              <Cell    ss:StyleID="""s62"""><Data
ss:Type="""String""">" + rs.Fields(x).Name+ "</Data></Cell>")
    Next
    txtstream.WriteLine("      </Row>")
    rs.MoveFirst()
    For y as Integer = 0 to rs.RecordCount-1
    txtstream.WriteLine("      <Row ss:AutoFitHeight="""0""">")
    For x as integer = 0 to rs.Fields.Count-1
    txtstream.WriteLine("                              <Cell    ss:StyleID="""s63"""><Data
ss:Type="""String""">" + rs.Fields(x).Value + "</Data></Cell>")
    Next
    txtstream.WriteLine("      </Row>")
    rs.MoveNext()
    Next
    txtstream.WriteLine("    </Table>")
    txtstream.WriteLine("  </Worksheet>")
    txtstream.WriteLine("</Workbook>")
    iret = txtstream.Close()
```

Vertical

```
    txtstream.WriteLine("<?xml version="""1.0"""?>")
    txtstream.WriteLine("<?mso-application progid="""Excel.Sheet"""?>")
    txtstream.WriteLine("<Workbook                 xmlns="""urn:schemas-microsoft-
com:office:spreadsheet"""    xmlns:o="""urn:schemas-microsoft-com:office:office"""
xmlns:x="""urn:schemas-microsoft-com:office:excel"""    xmlns:ss="""urn:schemas-
microsoft-com:office:spreadsheet"""    xmlns:html="""http://www.w3.org/TR/REC-
html40""">")
    txtstream.WriteLine("    <ExcelWorkbook   xmlns="""urn:schemas-microsoft-
com:office:excel""">")
    txtstream.WriteLine("           <WindowHeight>11835</WindowHeight>")
    txtstream.WriteLine("           <WindowWidth>18960</WindowWidth>")
    txtstream.WriteLine("           <WindowTopX>120</WindowTopX>")
```

```vb
txtstream.WriteLine("                    <WindowTopY>135</WindowTopY>")
txtstream.WriteLine("                    <ProtectStructure>False</ProtectStructure>")
txtstream.WriteLine("                    <ProtectWindows>False</ProtectWindows>")
txtstream.WriteLine(" </ExcelWorkbook>")
txtstream.WriteLine(" <Styles>")
txtstream.WriteLine("                    <Style ss:ID=""""s62"""">")
txtstream.WriteLine("                        <Borders/>")
txtstream.WriteLine("                        <Font
ss:FontName=""""Calibri""""          x:Family=""""Swiss""""          ss:Size=""""11""""
ss:Color=""""#000000"""" ss:Bold=""""1""""/>")
txtstream.WriteLine("                    </Style>")
txtstream.WriteLine("                    <Style ss:ID=""""s63"""">")
txtstream.WriteLine("                        <Alignment
ss:Horizontal=""""Left"""" ss:Vertical=""""Bottom"""" ss:Indent=""""2""""/>")
txtstream.WriteLine("                        <Font
ss:FontName=""""Verdana""""          x:Family=""""Swiss""""          ss:Size=""""7.7""""
ss:Color=""""#000000""""/>")
txtstream.WriteLine("                    </Style>")
txtstream.WriteLine(" </Styles>")
txtstream.WriteLine(" <Worksheet ss:Name=""""Win32_NetworkAdapter"""">")
txtstream.WriteLine("        <Table x:FullColumns=""""1""""  x:FullRows=""""1""""
ss:DefaultRowHeight=""""24.9375"""">")
txtstream.WriteLine("        <Column ss:AutoFitWidth=""""1"""" ss:Width=""""82.5""""
ss:Span=""""5""""/>")
For x as integer = 0 to rs.Fields.Count-1
txtstream.WriteLine("        <Row ss:AutoFitHeight=""""0"""">")
txtstream.WriteLine("                        <Cell  ss:StyleID=""""s62""""><Data
ss:Type=""""String"""">" + rs.Fields(x).Name+ "</Data></Cell>")
rs.MoveFirst()
For y as Integer = 0 to rs.RecordCount-1
txtstream.WriteLine("                        <Cell  ss:StyleID=""""s63""""><Data
ss:Type=""""String"""">" + rs.Fields(x).Value + "</Data></Cell>")
rs.MoveNext()
```

```
Next
txtstream.WriteLine("     </Row>")
Next
txtstream.WriteLine("   </Table>")
txtstream.WriteLine(" </Worksheet>")
txtstream.WriteLine("</Workbook>")
$iret = txtstream.Close()
```

Delimited Text Examples

BELOW ARE EXAMPLES OF ADO USING ODBC to create delimited text files.

Colon delimited horizontal text

```
Dim ws As Object  = CreateObject("WScript.Shell")
Dim fso As Object  = CreateObject("Scripting.FileSystemObject")
Dim txtstream as Object  = fso.OpenTextFile(ws.CurrentDirectory +
"\Products.txt", 2, True, -2)
Dim tstr
tstr= ""
For x = 0 To Rs.Fields.Count-1
   If (tstr <> "") Then
      tstr = tstr + ":"
   End If
   tstr = tstr  & rs.Fields(x).Name
Next
```

```
txtstream.Writeline(tstr)
tstr = ""
rs.MoveFirst()
For y as Integer = 0 to rs.RecordCount-1
  For x = 0 to rs.Fields.Count-1
    If (tstr <> "") Then
      tstr = tstr + ":"
    End If
    tstr = tstr & chr(34) & rs.Fields(x).Value & chr(34)
  Next
  txtstream.Writeline(tstr)
  tstr = ""
  rs.MoveNext()
Next
txtstream.Close
```

Colon Delimited vertical text

```
Dim ws As Object  = CreateObject("WScript.Shell")

Dim fso As Object  = CreateObject("Scripting.FileSystemObject")

Dim txtstream as Object  = fso.OpenTextFile(ws.CurrentDirectory +
"\Products.txt", 2, True, -2)

Dim tstr
tstr= ""
For x = 0 To Rs.Fields.Count-1
  tstr = rs.fields(x).Name
  rs.MoveFirst()
  for y as Integer = 0 to rs.RecordCount-1
    If (tstr <> "") Then
      tstr = tstr + ":"
    End If
    tstr = tstr & chr(34) & rs.Fields(x).Value & chr(34)
    rs.MoveNext()
  Next
  txtstream.Writeline(tstr)
  tstr = ""
Next
txtstream.Close
```

Coma delimited horizontal text

```
Dim ws As Object  = CreateObject("WScript.Shell")
Dim fso As Object  = CreateObject("Scripting.FileSystemObject")
Dim txtstream as Object  = fso.OpenTextFile(ws.CurrentDirectory +
"\Products.csv", 2, True, -2)
Dim tstr
tstr= ""
For x = 0 To Rs.Fields.Count-1
  If (tstr <> "") Then
    tstr = tstr + ","
  End If
  tstr = tstr  & rs.Fields(x).Name
Next


txtstream.Writeline(tstr)
tstr = ""
rs.MoveFirst()
For y as Integer = 0 to rs.RecordCount-1
  For x = 0 to rs.Fields.Count-1
    If (tstr <> "") Then
      tstr = tstr + ","
    End If
    tstr = tstr & chr(34) & rs.Fields(x).Value & chr(34)
  Next
  txtstream.Writeline(tstr)
  tstr = ""
  rs.MoveNext()
Next
txtstream.Close
```

Coma Delimited vertical text

```
Dim ws As Object  = CreateObject("WScript.Shell")
Dim fso As Object  = CreateObject("Scripting.FileSystemObject")
Dim txtstream as Object  = fso.OpenTextFile(ws.CurrentDirectory +
"\Products.txt", 2, True, -2)
Dim tstr
tstr= ""
```

```
For x = 0 To Rs.Fields.Count-1
  tstr = rs.fields(x).Name
  rs.MoveFirst()
  for y as Integer = 0 to rs.RecordCount-1
    If (tstr <> "") Then
      tstr = tstr + ","
    End If
    tstr = tstr & chr(34) & rs.Fields(x).Value & chr(34)
    rs.MoveNext()
  Next
  txtstream.Writeline(tstr)
  tstr = ""
Next
txtstream.Close
```

Exclamation delimited horizontal text

```
Dim ws As Object  = CreateObject("WScript.Shell")

Dim fso As Object  = CreateObject("Scripting.FileSystemObject")

Dim txtstream as Object  = fso.OpenTextFile(ws.CurrentDirectory +
"\Products.txt", 2, True, -2)
Dim tstr
tstr= ""
For x = 0 To Rs.Fields.Count-1
  If (tstr <> "") Then
    tstr = tstr + "!"
  End If
  tstr = tstr  & rs.Fields(x).Name
Next




txtstream.Writeline(tstr)
tstr = ""
rs.MoveFirst()
For y as Integer = 0 to rs.RecordCount-1
  For x = 0 to rs.Fields.Count-1
    If (tstr <> "") Then
```

```
            tstr = tstr + "!"
         End If
         tstr = tstr & chr(34) & rs.Fields(x).Value & chr(34)
      Next
      txtstream.Writeline(tstr)
      tstr = ""
      rs.MoveNext()
   Next
   txtstream.Close
```

Exclamation Delimited vertical text

```
Dim ws As Object  = CreateObject("WScript.Shell")

Dim fso As Object  = CreateObject("Scripting.FileSystemObject")

Dim txtstream as Object  = fso.OpenTextFile(ws.CurrentDirectory +
"\Products.txt", 2, True, -2)
Dim tstr
tstr= ""
For x = 0 To Rs.Fields.Count-1
   tstr = rs.fields(x).Name
   rs.MoveFirst()
   for y as Integer = 0 to rs.RecordCount-1
      If (tstr <> "") Then
         tstr = tstr + "!"
      End If
      tstr = tstr & chr(34) & rs.Fields(x).Value & chr(34)
      rs.MoveNext()
   Next
   txtstream.Writeline(tstr)
   tstr = ""
Next
txtstream.Close
```

Semi-colon delimited horizontal text

```
Dim ws As Object  = CreateObject("WScript.Shell")

Dim fso As Object  = CreateObject("Scripting.FileSystemObject")

Dim txtstream as Object  = fso.OpenTextFile(ws.CurrentDirectory +
"\Products.txt", 2, True, -2)
```

```
Dim tstr
tstr= ""
For x = 0 To Rs.Fields.Count-1
  If (tstr <> "") Then
    tstr = tstr + ";"
  End If
  tstr = tstr  & rs.Fields(x).Name
Next


txtstream.Writeline(tstr)
tstr = ""
rs.MoveFirst()
For y as Integer = 0 to rs.RecordCount-1
  For x = 0 to rs.Fields.Count-1
    If (tstr <> "") Then
      tstr = tstr + ";"
    End If
    tstr = tstr & chr(34) & rs.Fields(x).Value & chr(34)
  Next
  txtstream.Writeline(tstr)
  tstr = ""
  rs.MoveNext()
Next
txtstream.Close
```

Semi-colon Delimited vertical text

```
Dim ws As Object  = CreateObject("WScript.Shell")

Dim fso As Object  = CreateObject("Scripting.FileSystemObject")

Dim txtstream as Object  = fso.OpenTextFile(ws.CurrentDirectory +

"\Products.txt", 2, True, -2)

Dim tstr
tstr= ""
For x = 0 To Rs.Fields.Count-1
  tstr = rs.fields(x).Name
  rs.MoveFirst()
  for y as Integer = 0 to rs.RecordCount-1
    If (tstr <> "") Then
      tstr = tstr + ";"
    End If
    tstr = tstr & chr(34) & rs.Fields(x).Value & chr(34)
    rs.MoveNext()
  Next
```

```
        txtstream.Writeline(tstr)
        tstr = ""
     Next
     txtstream.Close
```

Tab delimited horizontal text

```
     Dim ws As Object  = CreateObject("WScript.Shell")
     Dim fso As Object  = CreateObject("Scripting.FileSystemObject")
     Dim txtstream as Object  = fso.OpenTextFile(ws.CurrentDirectory +
"\Products.txt", 2, True, -2)
     Dim tstr
     tstr= ""
     For x = 0 To Rs.Fields.Count-1
        If (tstr <> "") Then
           tstr = tstr + vbtab
        End If
        tstr = tstr  & rs.Fields(x).Name
     Next

     txtstream.Writeline(tstr)
     tstr = ""
     rs.MoveFirst()
     For y as Integer = 0 to rs.RecordCount-1
        For x = 0 to rs.Fields.Count-1
           If (tstr <> "") Then
              tstr = tstr + vbtab
           End If
           tstr = tstr & chr(34) & rs.Fields(x).Value & chr(34)
        Next
        txtstream.Writeline(tstr)
        tstr = ""
        rs.MoveNext()
     Next
     txtstream.Close
```

Tab delimited vertical text

```
     Dim ws As Object  = CreateObject("WScript.Shell")
     Dim fso As Object  = CreateObject("Scripting.FileSystemObject")
```

```
Dim txtstream as Object  = fso.OpenTextFile(ws.CurrentDirectory +
"\Products.txt", 2, True, -2)
    Dim tstr
    tstr= ""
    For x = 0 To Rs.Fields.Count-1
      tstr = rs.fields(x).Name
      rs.MoveFirst()
      for y as Integer = 0 to rs.RecordCount-1
        If (tstr <> "") Then
          tstr = tstr + vbtab
        End If
        tstr = tstr & chr(34) & rs.Fields(x).Value & chr(34)
        rs.MoveNext()
      Next
      txtstream.Writeline(tstr)
      tstr = ""
    Next
    txtstream.Close
```

Tilde delimited horizontal text

```
Dim ws As Object  = CreateObject("WScript.Shell")
Dim fso As Object  = CreateObject("Scripting.FileSystemObject")
Dim txtstream as Object  = fso.OpenTextFile(ws.CurrentDirectory +
"\Products.txt", 2, True, -2)
    Dim tstr
    tstr= ""
    For x = 0 To Rs.Fields.Count-1
      If (tstr <> "") Then
        tstr = tstr + "~"
      End If
      tstr = tstr  & rs.Fields(x).Name
    Next

    txtstream.Writeline(tstr)
    tstr = ""
    rs.MoveFirst()
    For y as Integer = 0 to rs.RecordCount-1
      For x = 0 to rs.Fields.Count-1
        If (tstr <> "") Then
          tstr = tstr + "~"
        End If
        tstr = tstr & chr(34) & rs.Fields(x).Value & chr(34)
```

```
        Next
        txtstream.Writeline(tstr)
        tstr = ""
        rs.MoveNext()
    Next
    txtstream.Close
```

Tilde delimited vertical text

```
Dim ws As Object  = CreateObject("WScript.Shell")

Dim fso As Object  = CreateObject("Scripting.FileSystemObject")

Dim txtstream as Object  = fso.OpenTextFile(ws.CurrentDirectory +
"\Products.txt", 2, True, -2)

Dim tstr
tstr= ""
For x = 0 To Rs.Fields.Count-1
    tstr = rs.fields(x).Name
    rs.MoveFirst()
    for y as Integer = 0 to rs.RecordCount-1
        If (tstr <> "") Then
            tstr = tstr + "~"
        End If
        tstr = tstr & chr(34) & rs.Fields(x).Value & chr(34)
        rs.MoveNext()
    Next
    txtstream.Writeline(tstr)
    tstr = ""
Next
txtstream.Close
```

Attribute XML Examples

B ELOW ARE EXAMPLES OF ADO USING ODBC AND CREATING ATTRIBUTE XML.

Create Attribute XML using A Text File

```
Dim ws As Object = CreateObject("WScript.Shell ")
Dim fso As Object = CreateObject("Scripting.FileSystemObject ")
Dim txtstream As Object = fso.OpenTextFile(ws.CurrentDirectory &
"\Products.xml", 2, true, -2)
txtstream.WriteLine("<?xml version='1.0' encoding='iso-8895-1'?>")
txtstream.WriteLine("<data>")
for each dr as System.Data.DataRow in ds.Tables(0).Rows
txtstream.WriteLine("<Products>")
For x = 0 To Rs.Fields.Count-1
Dim Name as String  = rs.fields(x).Name
Dim Value as String =  dr.Item(rs.fields(x).Name)
Dim tempstr as string = ""
tempstr = "<property Name=""" + Name + """ " & _
" DataType=""" + rs.Fields(x).Type.ToString() + """ " & _
"Value=""" + Value + """ />")
txtstream.WriteLine(tempstr)
```

```
    Next
    txtstream.WriteLine("</Products>")
    Next
    txtstream.WriteLine("</data>")
    txtstream.Close()
```

Create Attribute XML using the XML DOM

```
    Dim xmldoc As Object = CreateObject("MSXML2.DOMDocument")
    Dim pi As Object= xmldoc.CreateProcessingInstruction("xml", "version='1.0'
encoding='ISO-8859-1'")
    Dim oRoot As Object= xmldoc.CreateElement("data")
    xmldoc.AppendChild(pi)
    rs.MoveNext()
    For x as Integer = 0 to rs.RecordCount-1
      Dim oNode As Object= xmldoc.CreateNode(1, "Products", "")
      For x = 0 To Rs.Fields.Count-1
        Dim oNode1 As Object = xmldoc.CreateNode(1, "Property", "")
        Dim oAtt As Object = xmldoc.CreateAttribute("NAME")
        oAtt.Value = Rs.fields(x).Name
        oNode1.Attributes.SetNamedItem(oAtt)
        oAtt = xmldoc.CreateAttribute("DATATYPE")
        oAtt.Value = col.Datatype.Name
        oNode1.Attributes.SetNamedItem(oAtt)
        oAtt = xmldoc.CreateAttribute("SIZE")
        oAtt.Value = len(rs.Fields(x).Value)
        oNode1.Attributes.SetNamedItem(oAtt)
        oAtt = xmldoc.CreateAttribute("Value")
        oAtt.Value = rs.Fields(x).Value
        oNode1.Attributes.SetNamedItem(oAtt)
        oNode.AppendChild(oNode1)
      Next
```

```
        oRoot.AppendChild(oNode)
        rs.MoveNext()
Next
xmldoc.AppendChild(oRoot)
Dim ws As Object = CreateObject("WScript.Shell")
xmldoc.Save(ws.CurrentDirectory + "\Products.xml")
```

Element XML Examples

BELOW ARE EXAMPLES OF ADO USING ODBC.

Creating Element XML using A Text File

```
Dim ws As Object = CreateObject("WScript.Shell")
Dim fso As Object = CreateObject("Scripting.FileSystemObject")
Dim txtstream as Object = fso.OpenTextFile(ws.CurrentDirectory +
"\Products.txt", 2, True, -2)
txtstream.WriteLine("<?xml version='1.0' encoding='iso-8859-1'?>")
txtstream.WriteLine("<data>")
rs.MoveFirst()
for x as Integer = 0 to rs.RecordCount-1
    txtstream.WriteLine("<Products>")
    For x = 0 To Rs.Fields.Count-1
        txtstream.WriteLine("<" + rs.Fields(x).Name+ ">" + rs.Fields(x).Value
+ "</" + rs.Fields(x).Name+ ">")
```

```
            Next
            txtstream.WriteLine("</Products>")
            rs.MoveNext()
        Next
        txtstream.WriteLine("</data>")
        txtstream.close()
```

Creating Element XML using the XML DOM

```
        Dim xmldoc As Object = CreateObject("MSXML2.DOMDocument")
        Dim pi As Object= xmldoc.CreateProcessingInstruction("xml",
"version='1.0' encoding='ISO-8859-1'")
        Dim oRoot As Object= xmldoc.CreateElement("data")
        xmldoc.AppendChild(pi)
        rs.MoveFirst()
        For x as Integer = 0 to rs.RecordCount-1
            Dim oNode As Object= xmldoc.CreateNode(1, "Products", "")
            For x = 0 To Rs.Fields.Count-1
                Dim oNode1 As Object = xmldoc.CreateNode(1,
            rs.fields(x).Name, "")
                oNode.Text = Rs.Fields(x).Value
                oNode.AppendChild(oNode1)
            Next
            oRoot.AppendChild(oNode)
            rs.MoveNext()
        Next
        xmldoc.AppendChild(oRoot)

        Dim ws As Object = CreateObject("WScript.Shell")
        xmldoc.Save(ws.CurrentDirectory + "\Products.xml")
```

Element XML for XSL Examples

BELOW ARE EXAMPLES OF ADO USING ODBC.

Element XML for XSL using A Text File

```
Dim ws As Object  = CreateObject("WScript.Shell")
Dim fso As Object  = CreateObject("Scripting.FileSystemObject")
Dim txtstream as Object  = fso.OpenTextFile(ws.CurrentDirectory +
"\Products.txt", 2, True, -2)
txtstream.WriteLine("<?xml version='1.0' encoding='iso-8859-1'?>")
txtstream.WriteLine("<?xml-stylesheet    type='Text/xsl'    href='" +
ws.CurrentDirectory + "\Products.xsl"?>
txtstream.WriteLine("<data>")
rs.MoveFirst()
for x as Integer = 0 to rs.RecordCount-1
```

```
    txtstream.WriteLine("<Products>")
    For x = o To Rs.Fields.Count-1
         txtstream.WriteLine("<" + rs.Fields(x).Name+ ">" + rs.Fields(x).Value
+ "</" + rs.Fields(x).Name+ ">")
    Next
    txtstream.WriteLine("</Products>")
    rs.MoveNext()
Next
txtstream.WriteLine("</data>")
txtstream.close()
```

Element XML for XSL using a DOM

```
Dim xmldoc As Object = CreateObject("MSXML2.DOMDocument")
Dim pi As Object= xmldoc.CreateProcessingInstruction("xml", "version='1.0'
encoding='ISO-8859-1'")
Dim pii As Object = xmldoc.CreateProcessingInstruction("xml-stylesheet",
"type='text/xsl' href='Process.xsl'")
Dim oRoot As Object= xmldoc.CreateElement("data")
xmldoc.AppendChild(pi)
xmldoc.AppendChild(pii)

For x as Integer = 0 to rs.RecordCount-1
Dim oNode As Object= xmldoc.CreateNode(1, "Products", "")
    For x = o To Rs.Fields.Count-1
         Dim oNode1 As Object = xmldoc.CreateNode(1, rs.fields(x).Name, "")
         oNode.Text = Rs.Fields(x).Value
         oNode.AppendChild(oNode1)
    Next
    oRoot.AppendChild(oNode)
    rs.MoveNext()
Next
```

```
xmldoc.AppendChild(oRoot)
Dim ws As Object = CreateObject("WScript.Shell")
xmldoc.Save(ws.CurrentDirectory + "\Products.xml")
xmldoc = Nothing
```

Schema XML Examples

B ELOW ARE EXAMPLES OF ADO USING ODBC.

Schema XML using an Element XML File

```
Dim ws As Object = CreateObject("WScript.Shell")
Dim fso As Object = CreateObject("Scripting.FileSystemObject")
Dim txtstream as Object = fso.OpenTextFile(ws.CurrentDirectory +
"\Products.xml", 2, True, -2)
txtstream.WriteLine("<?xml version='1.0' encoding='iso-8859-1'?>")
txtstream.WriteLine("<data>")
rs.MoveFirst()
for x as Integer = 0 to rs.RecordCount-1
    txtstream.WriteLine("<Products>")
    For x = 0 To Rs.Fields.Count-1
        txtstream.WriteLine("<" + rs.Fields(x).Name+ ">" + rs.Fields(x).Value
+ "</" + rs.Fields(x).Name+ ">")
    Next
    txtstream.WriteLine("</Products>")
```

```
        rs.MoveNext()
    Next
    txtstream.WriteLine("</data>")
    txtstream.close()

    Dim rs1 As Object = CreateObject("ADODB.Recordset")
    rs1.ActiveConnection        =        "Provider=MSDAOSP;        Data
Source=msxml2.DSOControl"
    rs1.Open(ws.CurrentDirectory + "\Products.xml")

    If (fso.FileExists(ws.CurrentDirectory + "\Products_Schema.xml") = True)
Then
        fso.DeleteFile(ws.CurrentDirectory + "\Products_Schema.xml")
        End If

    rs.Save(ws.CurrentDirectory + "\Products_Schema.xml", 1)
```

Schema XML using the DOM

```
Dim xmldoc As Object = CreateObject("MSXML2.DOMDocument")
Dim pi As Object= xmldoc.CreateProcessingInstruction("xml", "version='1.0'
encoding='ISO-8859-1'")
Dim oRoot As Object= xmldoc.CreateElement("data")
xmldoc.AppendChild(pi)
For x as Integer = 0 to rs.RecordCount-1
    Dim oNode As Object= xmldoc.CreateNode(1, "Products", "")
    For x = 0 To Rs.Fields.Count-1
        Dim oNode1 As Object = xmldoc.CreateNode(1, rs.fields(x).Name, "")
        oNode.Text = Rs.Fields(x).Value
        oNode.AppendChild(oNode1)
    Next
    oRoot.AppendChild(oNode)
```

```
Next
xmldoc.AppendChild(oRoot)
Dim ws As Object = CreateObject("WScript.Shell")
xmldoc.Save(ws.CurrentDirectory + "\Products.xml")
xmldoc = Nothing


Dim rs1 As Object = CreateObject("ADODB.Recordset")
rs1.ActiveConnection = "Provider=MSDAOSP; Data Source=msxml2.DSOControl"
rs1.Open(ws.CurrentDirectory + "\Products.xml")

If (fso.FileExists(ws.CurrentDirectory + "\Products_Schema.xml") = True) Then
fso.DeleteFile(ws.CurrentDirectory + "\Products_Schema.xml")
End If

rs.Save(ws.CurrentDirectory + "\Products_Schema.xml", 1)
```

XSL Examples

BELOW ARE EXAMPLES OF ADO USING ODBC DRIVERS.

```
Dim ws As Object  = CreateObject("WScript.Shell")
Dim fso As Object  = CreateObject("Scripting.FileSystemObject")
Dim  txtstream  as  Object  =  fso.OpenTextFile(ws.CurrentDirectory  +
"\Products.xsl", 2, true, -2)
```

Single Line Horizontal Reports

```
txtstream.WriteLine("<?xml version='1.0' encoding='UTF-8'?>")
txtstream.WriteLine("<xsl:stylesheet                        version='1.0'
xmlns:xsl='http://www.w3.org/1999/XSL/Transform'>")
txtstream.WriteLine("<xsl:template match=""/"">")
txtstream.WriteLine("<html>")
txtstream.WriteLine("<head>")
txtstream.WriteLine("<title>Products</title>")
txtstream.WriteLine("</head>")
txtstream.WriteLine("<style type='text/css'>")
txtstream.WriteLine("th")
```

```
txtstream.WriteLine("{")
txtstream.WriteLine("    COLOR: darkred;")
txtstream.WriteLine("    BACKGROUND-COLOR: #eeeeee;")
txtstream.WriteLine("    FONT-FAMILY:font-family: Cambria, serif;")
txtstream.WriteLine("    FONT-SIZE: 12px;")
txtstream.WriteLine("    text-align: left;")
txtstream.WriteLine("    white-Space: nowrap='nowrap';")
txtstream.WriteLine("}")
txtstream.WriteLine("td")
txtstream.WriteLine("{")
txtstream.WriteLine("    COLOR: navy;")
txtstream.WriteLine("    BACKGROUND-COLOR: #eeeeee;")
txtstream.WriteLine("    FONT-FAMILY: font-family: Cambria, serif;")
txtstream.WriteLine("    FONT-SIZE: 12px;")
txtstream.WriteLine("    text-align: left;")
txtstream.WriteLine("    white-Space: nowrap='nowrap';")
txtstream.WriteLine("}")
txtstream.WriteLine("</style>")
txtstream.WriteLine("<body>")
txtstream.WriteLine("<table colspacing=""3"" colpadding=""3"">")


txtstream.WriteLine("<tr>")
For x As Integer = 0 to rs.Fields.count-1
txtstream.WriteLine("<th align='left' nowrap='true'>" + rs.Fields(x).Name+
"</th>")
next
txtstream.WriteLine("</tr>")
txtstream.WriteLine("<tr>")
For x As Integer = 0 to rs.Fields.count-1
txtstream.WriteLine("<td><xsl:value-of       select=""data/Products/"       +
rs.Fields(x).Name + """/></td>")
next
```

```
txtstream.WriteLine("</tr>")
txtstream.WriteLine("</table>")
txtstream.WriteLine("</body>")
txtstream.WriteLine("</html>")
txtstream.WriteLine("</xsl:template>")
txtstream.WriteLine("</xsl:stylesheet>")
txtstream.Close()
```

Multi Line Horizontal Reports

```
txtstream.WriteLine("<?xml version='1.0' encoding='UTF-8'?>")
txtstream.WriteLine("<xsl:stylesheet                          version='1.0'
xmlns:xsl='http://www.w3.org/1999/XSL/Transform'>")
txtstream.WriteLine("<xsl:template match=""""/""">")
txtstream.WriteLine("<html>")
txtstream.WriteLine("<head>")
txtstream.WriteLine("<title>Products</title>")
txtstream.WriteLine("</head>")
txtstream.WriteLine("<style type='text/css'>")
txtstream.WriteLine("th")
txtstream.WriteLine("{")
txtstream.WriteLine("    COLOR: darkred;")
txtstream.WriteLine("    BACKGROUND-COLOR: #eeeeee;")
txtstream.WriteLine("    FONT-FAMILY:font-family: Cambria, serif;")
txtstream.WriteLine("    FONT-SIZE: 12px;")
txtstream.WriteLine("    text-align: left;")
txtstream.WriteLine("    white-Space: nowrap='nowrap';")
txtstream.WriteLine("}")
txtstream.WriteLine("td")
txtstream.WriteLine("{")
txtstream.WriteLine("    COLOR: navy;")
txtstream.WriteLine("    BACKGROUND-COLOR: #eeeeee;")
txtstream.WriteLine("    FONT-FAMILY: font-family: Cambria, serif;")
```

```vb
txtstream.WriteLine("    FONT-SIZE: 12px;")
txtstream.WriteLine("    text-align: left;")
txtstream.WriteLine("    white-Space: nowrap='nowrap';")
txtstream.WriteLine("}")
txtstream.WriteLine("</style>")
txtstream.WriteLine("<body>")
txtstream.WriteLine("<table colspacing=""3"" colpadding=""3"">")


txtstream.WriteLine("<tr>")
For x As Integer = 0 to rs.Fields.count-1
txtstream.WriteLine("<th>" + rs.Fields(x).Name+ "</th>")
next
txtstream.WriteLine("</tr>")
txtstream.WriteLine("<xsl:for-each select=""data/Products"">")
txtstream.WriteLine("<tr>")
For x As Integer = 0 to rs.Fields.count-1
txtstream.WriteLine("<td><xsl:value-of  select="" " + rs.Fields(x).Name+ "
""/></td>")
txtstream.WriteLine("<td><xsl:value-of  select="""" + rs.Fields(x).Name +
""""/></td>")
next
txtstream.WriteLine("</tr>")
txtstream.WriteLine("</xsl:for-each>")
txtstream.WriteLine("</table>")
txtstream.WriteLine("</body>")
txtstream.WriteLine("</html>")
txtstream.WriteLine("</xsl:template>")
txtstream.WriteLine("</xsl:stylesheet>")
txtstream.Close()
```

```
txtstream.WriteLine("<?xml version='1.0' encoding='UTF-8'?>")
txtstream.WriteLine("<xsl:stylesheet                         version='1.0'
xmlns:xsl='http://www.w3.org/1999/XSL/Transform'>")
txtstream.WriteLine("<xsl:template match=""/"">")
txtstream.WriteLine("<html>")
txtstream.WriteLine("<head>")
txtstream.WriteLine("<title>Products</title>")
txtstream.WriteLine("</head>")
txtstream.WriteLine("<style type='text/css'>")
txtstream.WriteLine("th")
txtstream.WriteLine("{")
txtstream.WriteLine("   COLOR: darkred;")
txtstream.WriteLine("   BACKGROUND-COLOR: #eeeeee;")
txtstream.WriteLine("   FONT-FAMILY:font-family: Cambria, serif;")
txtstream.WriteLine("   FONT-SIZE: 12px;")
txtstream.WriteLine("   text-align: left;")
txtstream.WriteLine("   white-Space: nowrap='nowrap';")
txtstream.WriteLine("}")
txtstream.WriteLine("td")
txtstream.WriteLine("{")
txtstream.WriteLine("   COLOR: navy;")
txtstream.WriteLine("   BACKGROUND-COLOR: #eeeeee;")
txtstream.WriteLine("   FONT-FAMILY: font-family: Cambria, serif;")
txtstream.WriteLine("   FONT-SIZE: 12px;")
txtstream.WriteLine("   text-align: left;")
txtstream.WriteLine("   white-Space: nowrap='nowrap';")
txtstream.WriteLine("}")
txtstream.WriteLine("</style>")
txtstream.WriteLine("<body>")
txtstream.WriteLine("<table colspacing=""3"" colpadding=""3"">")
```

```vb
For x As Integer = 0 to rs.Fields.count-1
txtstream.WriteLine("<tr><th>" + rs.Fields(x).Name+ "</th>")
txtstream.WriteLine("<td><xsl:value-of        select=""data/Products/"      +
rs.Fields(x).Name + """/></td></tr>")
next
txtstream.WriteLine("</table>")
txtstream.WriteLine("</body>")
txtstream.WriteLine("</html>")
txtstream.WriteLine("</xsl:template>")
txtstream.WriteLine("</xsl:stylesheet>")
txtstream.Close()
```

Multi Line Vertical Report

```vb
txtstream.WriteLine("<?xml version='1.0' encoding='UTF-8'?>")
txtstream.WriteLine("<xsl:stylesheet                          version='1.0'
xmlns:xsl='http://www.w3.org/1999/XSL/Transform'>")
txtstream.WriteLine("<xsl:template match=""/"">")
txtstream.WriteLine("<html>")
txtstream.WriteLine("<head>")
txtstream.WriteLine("<title>Products</title>")
txtstream.WriteLine("</head>")
txtstream.WriteLine("<style type='text/css'>")
txtstream.WriteLine("th")
txtstream.WriteLine("{")
txtstream.WriteLine("    COLOR: darkred;")
txtstream.WriteLine("    BACKGROUND-COLOR: #eeeeee;")
txtstream.WriteLine("    FONT-FAMILY:font-family: Cambria, serif;")
txtstream.WriteLine("    FONT-SIZE: 12px;")
txtstream.WriteLine("    text-align: left;")
txtstream.WriteLine("    white-Space: nowrap='nowrap';")
```

```
txtstream.WriteLine("}")
txtstream.WriteLine("td")
txtstream.WriteLine("{")
txtstream.WriteLine("    COLOR: navy;")
txtstream.WriteLine("    BACKGROUND-COLOR: #eeeeee;")
txtstream.WriteLine("    FONT-FAMILY: font-family: Cambria, serif;")
txtstream.WriteLine("    FONT-SIZE: 12px;")
txtstream.WriteLine("    text-align: left;")
txtstream.WriteLine("    white-Space: nowrap='nowrap';")
txtstream.WriteLine("}")
txtstream.WriteLine("</style>")
txtstream.WriteLine("<body>")
txtstream.WriteLine("<table colspacing=""3"" colpadding=""3"">")

For x As Integer = 0 to rs.Fields.count-1
txtstream.WriteLine("<tr><th        align='left'        nowrap='true'>"        +
rs.Fields(x).Name+ "</th>")
    txtstream.WriteLine("<xsl:for-each select=""data/Products""><td align='left'
nowrap='true'><xsl:value-of select=""" + rs.Fields(x).Name + """/></td></xsl:for-
each></tr>")
next
txtstream.WriteLine("</table>")
txtstream.WriteLine("</body>")
txtstream.WriteLine("</html>")
txtstream.WriteLine("</xsl:template>")
txtstream.WriteLine("</xsl:stylesheet>")
txtstream.Close()
```

Single Line Horizontal Table

```
txtstream.WriteLine("<?xml version='1.0' encoding='UTF-8'?>")
txtstream.WriteLine("<xsl:stylesheet                          version='1.0'
xmlns:xsl='http://www.w3.org/1999/XSL/Transform'>")
```

```
txtstream.WriteLine("<xsl:template match=""/"">")
txtstream.WriteLine("<html>")
txtstream.WriteLine("<head>")
txtstream.WriteLine("<title>Products</title>")
txtstream.WriteLine("</head>")
txtstream.WriteLine("<style type='text/css'>")
txtstream.WriteLine("th")
txtstream.WriteLine("{")
txtstream.WriteLine("   COLOR: darkred;")
txtstream.WriteLine("   BACKGROUND-COLOR: #eeeeee;")
txtstream.WriteLine("   FONT-FAMILY:font-family: Cambria, serif;")
txtstream.WriteLine("   FONT-SIZE: 12px;")
txtstream.WriteLine("   text-align: left;")
txtstream.WriteLine("   white-Space: nowrap='nowrap';")
txtstream.WriteLine("}")
txtstream.WriteLine("td")
txtstream.WriteLine("{")
txtstream.WriteLine("   COLOR: navy;")
txtstream.WriteLine("   BACKGROUND-COLOR: #eeeeee;")
txtstream.WriteLine("   FONT-FAMILY: font-family: Cambria, serif;")
txtstream.WriteLine("   FONT-SIZE: 12px;")
txtstream.WriteLine("   text-align: left;")
txtstream.WriteLine("   white-Space: nowrap='nowrap';")
txtstream.WriteLine("}")
txtstream.WriteLine("</style>")
txtstream.WriteLine("<body>")
txtstream.WriteLine("<table     style='border:Double;border-width:1px;border-color:navy;' rules='all' frames='both' cellpadding='2' cellspacing='2'>")


txtstream.WriteLine("<tr>")
For x As Integer = 0 to rs.Fields.count-1
```

```
txtstream.WriteLine("<th align='left' nowrap='true'>" + rs.Fields(x).Name+
"</th>")
next
txtstream.WriteLine("</tr>")
txtstream.WriteLine("<tr>")
For x As Integer = 0 to rs.Fields.count-1
txtstream.WriteLine("<td><xsl:value-of        select=""data/Products/"      +
rs.Fields(x).Name + """/></td>")
next
txtstream.WriteLine("</tr>")
txtstream.WriteLine("</table>")
txtstream.WriteLine("</body>")
txtstream.WriteLine("</html>")
txtstream.WriteLine("</xsl:template>")
txtstream.WriteLine("</xsl:stylesheet>")
txtstream.Close()
```

Multi Line Horizontal Table

```
txtstream.WriteLine("<?xml version='1.0' encoding='UTF-8'?>")
txtstream.WriteLine("<xsl:stylesheet                               version='1.0'
xmlns:xsl='http://www.w3.org/1999/XSL/Transform'>")
txtstream.WriteLine("<xsl:template match=""/"">")
txtstream.WriteLine("<html>")
txtstream.WriteLine("<head>")
txtstream.WriteLine("<title>Products</title>")
txtstream.WriteLine("</head>")
txtstream.WriteLine("<style type='text/css'>")
txtstream.WriteLine("th")
txtstream.WriteLine("{")
txtstream.WriteLine("   COLOR: darkred;")
txtstream.WriteLine("   BACKGROUND-COLOR: #eeeeee;")
```

```
txtstream.WriteLine("   FONT-FAMILY:font-family: Cambria, serif;")
txtstream.WriteLine("   FONT-SIZE: 12px;")
txtstream.WriteLine("   text-align: left;")
txtstream.WriteLine("   white-Space: nowrap='nowrap';")
txtstream.WriteLine("}")
txtstream.WriteLine("td")
txtstream.WriteLine("{")
txtstream.WriteLine("   COLOR: navy;")
txtstream.WriteLine("   BACKGROUND-COLOR: #eeeeee;")
txtstream.WriteLine("   FONT-FAMILY: font-family: Cambria, serif;")
txtstream.WriteLine("   FONT-SIZE: 12px;")
txtstream.WriteLine("   text-align: left;")
txtstream.WriteLine("   white-Space: nowrap='nowrap';")
txtstream.WriteLine("}")
txtstream.WriteLine("</style>")
txtstream.WriteLine("<body>")
txtstream.WriteLine("<table    style='border:Double;border-width:1px;border-color:navy;' rules='all' frames='both' cellpadding='2' cellspacing='2'>")


txtstream.WriteLine("<tr>")
For x As Integer = 0 to rs.Fields.count-1
txtstream.WriteLine("<th>" + rs.Fields(x).Name+ "</th>")
next
txtstream.WriteLine("</tr>")
txtstream.WriteLine("<xsl:for-each select=""data/Products"">")
txtstream.WriteLine("<tr>")
For x As Integer = 0 to rs.Fields.count-1
txtstream.WriteLine("<td><xsl:value-of select="" " + rs.Fields(x).Name+ "
""/></td>")
txtstream.WriteLine("<td><xsl:value-of select=""" + rs.Fields(x).Name +
"""/></td>")
next
```

```
txtstream.WriteLine("</tr>")
txtstream.WriteLine("</xsl:for-each>")
txtstream.WriteLine("</table>")
txtstream.WriteLine("</body>")
txtstream.WriteLine("</html>")
txtstream.WriteLine("</xsl:template>")
txtstream.WriteLine("</xsl:stylesheet>")
txtstream.Close()
```

Single Line Vertical

```
txtstream.WriteLine("<?xml version='1.0' encoding='UTF-8'?>")
txtstream.WriteLine("<xsl:stylesheet                          version='1.0'
xmlns:xsl='http://www.w3.org/1999/XSL/Transform'>")
txtstream.WriteLine("<xsl:template match=""/"">")
txtstream.WriteLine("<html>")
txtstream.WriteLine("<head>")
txtstream.WriteLine("<title>Products</title>")
txtstream.WriteLine("</head>")
txtstream.WriteLine("<style type='text/css'>")
txtstream.WriteLine("th")
txtstream.WriteLine("{")
txtstream.WriteLine("   COLOR: darkred;")
txtstream.WriteLine("   BACKGROUND-COLOR: #eeeeee;")
txtstream.WriteLine("   FONT-FAMILY:font-family: Cambria, serif;")
txtstream.WriteLine("   FONT-SIZE: 12px;")
txtstream.WriteLine("   text-align: left;")
txtstream.WriteLine("   white-Space: nowrap='nowrap';")
txtstream.WriteLine("}")
txtstream.WriteLine("td")
txtstream.WriteLine("{")
txtstream.WriteLine("   COLOR: navy;")
txtstream.WriteLine("   BACKGROUND-COLOR: #eeeeee;")
```

```
txtstream.WriteLine("    FONT-FAMILY: font-family: Cambria, serif;")
txtstream.WriteLine("    FONT-SIZE: 12px;")
txtstream.WriteLine("    text-align: left;")
txtstream.WriteLine("    white-Space: nowrap='nowrap';")
txtstream.WriteLine("}")
txtstream.WriteLine("</style>")
txtstream.WriteLine("<body>")
txtstream.WriteLine("<table    style='border:Double;border-width:1px;border-color:navy;' rules='all' frames='both' cellpadding='2' cellspacing='2'>")


For x As Integer = 0 to rs.Fields.count-1
txtstream.WriteLine("<tr><th>" + rs.Fields(x).Name+ "</th>")
txtstream.WriteLine("<td><xsl:value-of    select=""data/Products/" + rs.Fields(x).Name + """/></td></tr>")
next
txtstream.WriteLine("</table>")
txtstream.WriteLine("</body>")
txtstream.WriteLine("</html>")
txtstream.WriteLine("</xsl:template>")
txtstream.WriteLine("</xsl:stylesheet>")
txtstream.Close()
```

Multi Line Vertical

```
txtstream.WriteLine("<?xml version='1.0' encoding='UTF-8'?>")
txtstream.WriteLine("<xsl:stylesheet                          version='1.0' xmlns:xsl='http://www.w3.org/1999/XSL/Transform'>")
txtstream.WriteLine("<xsl:template match=""/"">")
txtstream.WriteLine("<html>")
txtstream.WriteLine("<head>")
txtstream.WriteLine("<title>Products</title>")
```

```
txtstream.WriteLine("</head>")
txtstream.WriteLine("<style type='text/css'>")
txtstream.WriteLine("th")
txtstream.WriteLine("{")
txtstream.WriteLine("    COLOR: darkred;")
txtstream.WriteLine("    BACKGROUND-COLOR: #eeeeee;")
txtstream.WriteLine("    FONT-FAMILY:font-family: Cambria, serif;")
txtstream.WriteLine("    FONT-SIZE: 12px;")
txtstream.WriteLine("    text-align: left;")
txtstream.WriteLine("    white-Space: nowrap='nowrap';")
txtstream.WriteLine("}")
txtstream.WriteLine("td")
txtstream.WriteLine("{")
txtstream.WriteLine("    COLOR: navy;")
txtstream.WriteLine("    BACKGROUND-COLOR: #eeeeee;")
txtstream.WriteLine("    FONT-FAMILY: font-family: Cambria, serif;")
txtstream.WriteLine("    FONT-SIZE: 12px;")
txtstream.WriteLine("    text-align: left;")
txtstream.WriteLine("    white-Space: nowrap='nowrap';")
txtstream.WriteLine("}")
txtstream.WriteLine("</style>")
txtstream.WriteLine("<body>")
txtstream.WriteLine("<table    style='border:Double;border-width:1px;border-
color:navy;' rules='all' frames='both' cellpadding='2' cellspacing='2'>")

For x As Integer = 0 to rs.Fields.count-1
txtstream.WriteLine("<tr><th       align='left'       nowrap='true'>"       +
rs.Fields(x).Name+ "</th>")
txtstream.WriteLine("<xsl:for-each select=""data/Products""><td align='left'
nowrap='true'><xsl:value-of select=""" + rs.Fields(x).Name + """/></td></xsl:for-
each></tr>")
next
txtstream.WriteLine("</table>")
```

```
txtstream.WriteLine("</body>")
txtstream.WriteLine("</html>")
txtstream.WriteLine("</xsl:template>")
txtstream.WriteLine("</xsl:stylesheet>")
txtstream.Close()
```

Stylesheets
Some CSS Decorated Fuel for Thought

These are here for your consideration.

NONE

```
txtstream.WriteLine("<style type='text/css'>")
txtstream.WriteLine("th")
txtstream.WriteLine("")
txtstream.WriteLine("   COLOR: white;")
txtstream.WriteLine(" Next")
txtstream.WriteLine("td")
txtstream.WriteLine("")
txtstream.WriteLine("   COLOR: white;")
txtstream.WriteLine(" Next")
txtstream.WriteLine("</style>")
```

BLACK AND WHITE TEXT

```
txtstream.WriteLine("<style type='text/css'>")
txtstream.WriteLine("th")
```

```
txtstream.WriteLine("")
txtstream.WriteLine("    COLOR: white;")
txtstream.WriteLine("    BACKGROUND-COLOR: black;")
txtstream.WriteLine("    FONT-FAMILY:font-family: Cambria, serif;")
txtstream.WriteLine("    FONT-SIZE: 12px;")
txtstream.WriteLine("    text-align: left;")
txtstream.WriteLine("    white-Space: nowrap;")
txtstream.WriteLine(" Next")
txtstream.WriteLine("td")
txtstream.WriteLine("")
txtstream.WriteLine("    COLOR: white;")
txtstream.WriteLine("    BACKGROUND-COLOR: black;")
txtstream.WriteLine("    FONT-FAMILY: font-family: Cambria, serif;")
txtstream.WriteLine("    FONT-SIZE: 12px;")
txtstream.WriteLine("    text-align: left;")
txtstream.WriteLine("    white-Space: nowrap;")
txtstream.WriteLine(" Next")
txtstream.WriteLine("div")
txtstream.WriteLine("")
txtstream.WriteLine("    COLOR: white;")
txtstream.WriteLine("    BACKGROUND-COLOR: black;")
txtstream.WriteLine("    FONT-FAMILY: font-family: Cambria, serif;")
txtstream.WriteLine("    FONT-SIZE: 10px;")
txtstream.WriteLine("    text-align: left;")
txtstream.WriteLine("    white-Space: nowrap;")
txtstream.WriteLine(" Next")
txtstream.WriteLine("span")
txtstream.WriteLine("")
txtstream.WriteLine("    COLOR: white;")
txtstream.WriteLine("    BACKGROUND-COLOR: black;")
txtstream.WriteLine("    FONT-FAMILY: font-family: Cambria, serif;")
txtstream.WriteLine("    FONT-SIZE: 10px;")
txtstream.WriteLine("    text-align: left;")
```

```
txtstream.WriteLine("    white-Space: nowrap;")
txtstream.WriteLine("    display:inline-block;")
txtstream.WriteLine("    width: 100%;")
txtstream.WriteLine(" Next")
txtstream.WriteLine("textarea")
txtstream.WriteLine("")
txtstream.WriteLine("    COLOR: white;")
txtstream.WriteLine("    BACKGROUND-COLOR: black;")
txtstream.WriteLine("    FONT-FAMILY: font-family: Cambria, serif;")
txtstream.WriteLine("    FONT-SIZE: 10px;")
txtstream.WriteLine("    text-align: left;")
txtstream.WriteLine("    white-Space: nowrap;")
txtstream.WriteLine("    width: 100%;")
txtstream.WriteLine(" Next")
txtstream.WriteLine("select")
txtstream.WriteLine("")
txtstream.WriteLine("    COLOR: white;")
txtstream.WriteLine("    BACKGROUND-COLOR: black;")
txtstream.WriteLine("    FONT-FAMILY: font-family: Cambria, serif;")
txtstream.WriteLine("    FONT-SIZE: 10px;")
txtstream.WriteLine("    text-align: left;")
txtstream.WriteLine("    white-Space: nowrap;")
txtstream.WriteLine("    width: 100%;")
txtstream.WriteLine(" Next")
txtstream.WriteLine("input")
txtstream.WriteLine("")
txtstream.WriteLine("    COLOR: white;")
txtstream.WriteLine("    BACKGROUND-COLOR: black;")
txtstream.WriteLine("    FONT-FAMILY: font-family: Cambria, serif;")
txtstream.WriteLine("    FONT-SIZE: 12px;")
txtstream.WriteLine("    text-align: left;")
txtstream.WriteLine("    display:table-cell;")
txtstream.WriteLine("    white-Space: nowrap;")
```

```
txtstream.WriteLine(" Next")
txtstream.WriteLine("h1 ")
txtstream.WriteLine("color: antiquewhite;")
txtstream.WriteLine("text-shadow: 1px 1px 1px black;")
txtstream.WriteLine("padding: 3px;")
txtstream.WriteLine("text-align: center;")
txtstream.WriteLine("box-shadow: inSet 2px 2px 5px rgba(0,0,0,0.5), inSet -
2px -2px 5px rgba(255,255,255,0.5);")
txtstream.WriteLine(" Next")
txtstream.WriteLine("</style>")
```

COLORED TEXT

```
txtstream.WriteLine("<style type='text/css'>")
txtstream.WriteLine("th")
txtstream.WriteLine("")
txtstream.WriteLine("   COLOR: darkred;")
txtstream.WriteLine("   BACKGROUND-COLOR: #eeeeee;")
txtstream.WriteLine("   FONT-FAMILY:font-family: Cambria, serif;")
txtstream.WriteLine("   FONT-SIZE: 12px;")
txtstream.WriteLine("   text-align: left;")
txtstream.WriteLine("   white-Space: nowrap;")
txtstream.WriteLine(" Next")
txtstream.WriteLine("td")
txtstream.WriteLine("")
txtstream.WriteLine("   COLOR: navy;")
txtstream.WriteLine("   BACKGROUND-COLOR: #eeeeee;")
txtstream.WriteLine("   FONT-FAMILY: font-family: Cambria, serif;")
txtstream.WriteLine("   FONT-SIZE: 12px;")
txtstream.WriteLine("   text-align: left;")
txtstream.WriteLine("   white-Space: nowrap;")
txtstream.WriteLine(" Next")
txtstream.WriteLine("div")
txtstream.WriteLine("")
```

```
txtstream.WriteLine("    COLOR: white;")
txtstream.WriteLine("    BACKGROUND-COLOR: navy;")
txtstream.WriteLine("    FONT-FAMILY: font-family: Cambria, serif;")
txtstream.WriteLine("    FONT-SIZE: 10px;")
txtstream.WriteLine("    text-align: left;")
txtstream.WriteLine("    white-Space: nowrap;")
txtstream.WriteLine(" Next")
txtstream.WriteLine("span")
txtstream.WriteLine("")
txtstream.WriteLine("    COLOR: white;")
txtstream.WriteLine("    BACKGROUND-COLOR: navy;")
txtstream.WriteLine("    FONT-FAMILY: font-family: Cambria, serif;")
txtstream.WriteLine("    FONT-SIZE: 10px;")
txtstream.WriteLine("    text-align: left;")
txtstream.WriteLine("    white-Space: nowrap;")
txtstream.WriteLine("    display:inline-block;")
txtstream.WriteLine("    width: 100%;")
txtstream.WriteLine(" Next")
txtstream.WriteLine("textarea")
txtstream.WriteLine("")
txtstream.WriteLine("    COLOR: white;")
txtstream.WriteLine("    BACKGROUND-COLOR: navy;")
txtstream.WriteLine("    FONT-FAMILY: font-family: Cambria, serif;")
txtstream.WriteLine("    FONT-SIZE: 10px;")
txtstream.WriteLine("    text-align: left;")
txtstream.WriteLine("    white-Space: nowrap;")
txtstream.WriteLine("    width: 100%;")
txtstream.WriteLine(" Next")
txtstream.WriteLine("select")
txtstream.WriteLine("")
txtstream.WriteLine("    COLOR: white;")
txtstream.WriteLine("    BACKGROUND-COLOR: navy;")
txtstream.WriteLine("    FONT-FAMILY: font-family: Cambria, serif;")
```

```
txtstream.WriteLine("    FONT-SIZE: 10px;")
txtstream.WriteLine("    text-align: left;")
txtstream.WriteLine("    white-Space: nowrap;")
txtstream.WriteLine("    width: 100%;")
txtstream.WriteLine(" Next")
txtstream.WriteLine("input")
txtstream.WriteLine("")
txtstream.WriteLine("    COLOR: white;")
txtstream.WriteLine("    BACKGROUND-COLOR: navy;")
txtstream.WriteLine("    FONT-FAMILY: font-family: Cambria, serif;")
txtstream.WriteLine("    FONT-SIZE: 12px;")
txtstream.WriteLine("    text-align: left;")
txtstream.WriteLine("    display:table-cell;")
txtstream.WriteLine("    white-Space: nowrap;")
txtstream.WriteLine(" Next")
txtstream.WriteLine("h1 ")
txtstream.WriteLine("color: antiquewhite;")
txtstream.WriteLine("text-shadow: 1px 1px 1px black;")
txtstream.WriteLine("padding: 3px;")
txtstream.WriteLine("text-align: center;")
txtstream.WriteLine("box-shadow: inSet 2px 2px 5px rgba(0,0,0,0.5), inSet -2px -2px 5px rgba(255,255,255,0.5);")
txtstream.WriteLine(" Next")
txtstream.WriteLine("</style>")
```

OSCILLATING ROW COLORS

```
txtstream.WriteLine("<style>")
txtstream.WriteLine("th")
txtstream.WriteLine("")
txtstream.WriteLine("    COLOR: white;")
```

```
txtstream.WriteLine("   BACKGROUND-COLOR: navy;")
txtstream.WriteLine("   FONT-FAMILY:font-family: Cambria, serif;")
txtstream.WriteLine("   FONT-SIZE: 12px;")
txtstream.WriteLine("   text-align: left;")
txtstream.WriteLine("   white-Space: nowrap;")
txtstream.WriteLine(" Next")
txtstream.WriteLine("td")
txtstream.WriteLine("")
txtstream.WriteLine("   COLOR: navy;")
txtstream.WriteLine("   FONT-FAMILY: font-family: Cambria, serif;")
txtstream.WriteLine("   FONT-SIZE: 12px;")
txtstream.WriteLine("   text-align: left;")
txtstream.WriteLine("   white-Space: nowrap;")
txtstream.WriteLine(" Next")
txtstream.WriteLine("div")
txtstream.WriteLine("")
txtstream.WriteLine("   COLOR: navy;")
txtstream.WriteLine("   FONT-FAMILY: font-family: Cambria, serif;")
txtstream.WriteLine("   FONT-SIZE: 12px;")
txtstream.WriteLine("   text-align: left;")
txtstream.WriteLine("   white-Space: nowrap;")
txtstream.WriteLine(" Next")
txtstream.WriteLine("span")
txtstream.WriteLine("")
txtstream.WriteLine("   COLOR: navy;")
txtstream.WriteLine("   FONT-FAMILY: font-family: Cambria, serif;")
txtstream.WriteLine("   FONT-SIZE: 12px;")
txtstream.WriteLine("   text-align: left;")
txtstream.WriteLine("   white-Space: nowrap;")
txtstream.WriteLine("   width: 100%;")
txtstream.WriteLine(" Next")
txtstream.WriteLine("textarea")
txtstream.WriteLine("")
```

```
txtstream.WriteLine("    COLOR: navy;")
txtstream.WriteLine("    FONT-FAMILY: font-family: Cambria, serif;")
txtstream.WriteLine("    FONT-SIZE: 12px;")
txtstream.WriteLine("    text-align: left;")
txtstream.WriteLine("    white-Space: nowrap;")
txtstream.WriteLine("    display:inline-block;")
txtstream.WriteLine("    width: 100%;")
txtstream.WriteLine(" Next")
txtstream.WriteLine("select")
txtstream.WriteLine("")
txtstream.WriteLine("    COLOR: navy;")
txtstream.WriteLine("    FONT-FAMILY: font-family: Cambria, serif;")
txtstream.WriteLine("    FONT-SIZE: 10px;")
txtstream.WriteLine("    text-align: left;")
txtstream.WriteLine("    white-Space: nowrap;")
txtstream.WriteLine("    display:inline-block;")
txtstream.WriteLine("    width: 100%;")
txtstream.WriteLine(" Next")
txtstream.WriteLine("input")
txtstream.WriteLine("")
txtstream.WriteLine("    COLOR: navy;")
txtstream.WriteLine("    FONT-FAMILY: font-family: Cambria, serif;")
txtstream.WriteLine("    FONT-SIZE: 12px;")
txtstream.WriteLine("    text-align: left;")
txtstream.WriteLine("    display:table-cell;")
txtstream.WriteLine("    white-Space: nowrap;")
txtstream.WriteLine(" Next")
txtstream.WriteLine("h1 ")
txtstream.WriteLine("color: antiquewhite;")
txtstream.WriteLine("text-shadow: 1px 1px 1px black;")
txtstream.WriteLine("padding: 3px;")
txtstream.WriteLine("text-align: center;")
```

txtstream.WriteLine("box-shadow: inSet 2px 2px 5px rgba(0,0,0,0.5), inSet -2px -2px 5px rgba(255,255,255,0.5);")

txtstream.WriteLine(" Next")

txtstream.WriteLine("tr:nth-child(even)background-color:#f2f2f2; Next")

txtstream.WriteLine("tr:nth-child(odd)background-color:#cccccc; color:#f2f2f2; Next")

txtstream.WriteLine("</style>")

GHOST DECORATED

txtstream.WriteLine("<style type='text/css'>")

txtstream.WriteLine("th")

txtstream.WriteLine("")

txtstream.WriteLine("   COLOR: black;")

txtstream.WriteLine("   BACKGROUND-COLOR: white;")

txtstream.WriteLine("   FONT-FAMILY:font-family: Cambria, serif;")

txtstream.WriteLine("   FONT-SIZE: 12px;")

txtstream.WriteLine("   text-align: left;")

txtstream.WriteLine("   white-Space: nowrap;")

txtstream.WriteLine(" Next")

txtstream.WriteLine("td")

txtstream.WriteLine("")

txtstream.WriteLine("   COLOR: black;")

txtstream.WriteLine("   BACKGROUND-COLOR: white;")

txtstream.WriteLine("   FONT-FAMILY: font-family: Cambria, serif;")

txtstream.WriteLine("   FONT-SIZE: 12px;")

txtstream.WriteLine("   text-align: left;")

txtstream.WriteLine("   white-Space: nowrap;")

txtstream.WriteLine(" Next")

txtstream.WriteLine("div")

txtstream.WriteLine("")

txtstream.WriteLine("   COLOR: black;")

txtstream.WriteLine("   BACKGROUND-COLOR: white;")

```
txtstream.WriteLine(" FONT-FAMILY: font-family: Cambria, serif;")
txtstream.WriteLine(" FONT-SIZE: 10px;")
txtstream.WriteLine(" text-align: left;")
txtstream.WriteLine(" white-Space: nowrap;")
txtstream.WriteLine(" Next")
txtstream.WriteLine("span")
txtstream.WriteLine("")
txtstream.WriteLine(" COLOR: black;")
txtstream.WriteLine(" BACKGROUND-COLOR: white;")
txtstream.WriteLine(" FONT-FAMILY: font-family: Cambria, serif;")
txtstream.WriteLine(" FONT-SIZE: 10px;")
txtstream.WriteLine(" text-align: left;")
txtstream.WriteLine(" white-Space: nowrap;")
txtstream.WriteLine(" display:inline-block;")
txtstream.WriteLine(" width: 100%;")
txtstream.WriteLine(" Next")
txtstream.WriteLine("textarea")
txtstream.WriteLine("")
txtstream.WriteLine(" COLOR: black;")
txtstream.WriteLine(" BACKGROUND-COLOR: white;")
txtstream.WriteLine(" FONT-FAMILY: font-family: Cambria, serif;")
txtstream.WriteLine(" FONT-SIZE: 10px;")
txtstream.WriteLine(" text-align: left;")
txtstream.WriteLine(" white-Space: nowrap;")
txtstream.WriteLine(" width: 100%;")
txtstream.WriteLine(" Next")
txtstream.WriteLine("select")
txtstream.WriteLine("")
txtstream.WriteLine(" COLOR: black;")
txtstream.WriteLine(" BACKGROUND-COLOR: white;")
txtstream.WriteLine(" FONT-FAMILY: font-family: Cambria, serif;")
txtstream.WriteLine(" FONT-SIZE: 10px;")
txtstream.WriteLine(" text-align: left;")
```

```
txtstream.WriteLine("    white-Space: nowrap;")
txtstream.WriteLine("    width: 100%;")
txtstream.WriteLine(" Next")
txtstream.WriteLine("input")
txtstream.WriteLine("")
txtstream.WriteLine("    COLOR: black;")
txtstream.WriteLine("    BACKGROUND-COLOR: white;")
txtstream.WriteLine("    FONT-FAMILY: font-family: Cambria, serif;")
txtstream.WriteLine("    FONT-SIZE: 12px;")
txtstream.WriteLine("    text-align: left;")
txtstream.WriteLine("    display:table-cell;")
txtstream.WriteLine("    white-Space: nowrap;")
txtstream.WriteLine(" Next")
txtstream.WriteLine("h1 ")
txtstream.WriteLine("color: antiquewhite;")
txtstream.WriteLine("text-shadow: 1px 1px 1px black;")
txtstream.WriteLine("padding: 3px;")
txtstream.WriteLine("text-align: center;")
txtstream.WriteLine("box-shadow: inSet 2px 2px 5px rgba(0,0,0,0.5), inSet -
2px -2px 5px rgba(255,255,255,0.5);")
txtstream.WriteLine(" Next")
txtstream.WriteLine("</style>")
```

3D

```
txtstream.WriteLine("<style type='text/css'>")
txtstream.WriteLine("body")
txtstream.WriteLine("")
txtstream.WriteLine("    PADDING-RIGHT: 0px;")
txtstream.WriteLine("    PADDING-LEFT: 0px;")
txtstream.WriteLine("    PADDING-BOTTOM: 0px;")
txtstream.WriteLine("    MARGIN: 0px;")
```

```
txtstream.WriteLine("   COLOR: #333;")
txtstream.WriteLine("   PADDING-TOP: 0px;")
txtstream.WriteLine("   FONT-FAMILY: verdana, arial, helvetica, sans-serif;")
txtstream.WriteLine(" Next")
txtstream.WriteLine("table")
txtstream.WriteLine(""")
txtstream.WriteLine("   BORDER-RIGHT: #999999 3px solid;")
txtstream.WriteLine("   PADDING-RIGHT: 6px;")
txtstream.WriteLine("   PADDING-LEFT: 6px;")
txtstream.WriteLine("   FONT-WEIGHT: Bold;")
txtstream.WriteLine("   FONT-SIZE: 14px;")
txtstream.WriteLine("   PADDING-BOTTOM: 6px;")
txtstream.WriteLine("   COLOR: Peru;")
txtstream.WriteLine("   LINE-HEIGHT: 14px;")
txtstream.WriteLine("   PADDING-TOP: 6px;")
txtstream.WriteLine("   BORDER-BOTTOM: #999 1px solid;")
txtstream.WriteLine("   BACKGROUND-COLOR: #eeeeee;")
txtstream.WriteLine("   FONT-FAMILY: verdana, arial, helvetica, sans-serif;")
txtstream.WriteLine("   FONT-SIZE: 12px;")
txtstream.WriteLine(" Next")
txtstream.WriteLine("th")
txtstream.WriteLine(""")
txtstream.WriteLine("   BORDER-RIGHT: #999999 3px solid;")
txtstream.WriteLine("   PADDING-RIGHT: 6px;")
txtstream.WriteLine("   PADDING-LEFT: 6px;")
txtstream.WriteLine("   FONT-WEIGHT: Bold;")
txtstream.WriteLine("   FONT-SIZE: 14px;")
txtstream.WriteLine("   PADDING-BOTTOM: 6px;")
txtstream.WriteLine("   COLOR: darkred;")
txtstream.WriteLine("   LINE-HEIGHT: 14px;")
txtstream.WriteLine("   PADDING-TOP: 6px;")
txtstream.WriteLine("   BORDER-BOTTOM: #999 1px solid;")
txtstream.WriteLine("   BACKGROUND-COLOR: #eeeeee;")
```

```
txtstream.WriteLine("    FONT-FAMILY:font-family: Cambria, serif;")
txtstream.WriteLine("    FONT-SIZE: 12px;")
txtstream.WriteLine("    text-align: left;")
txtstream.WriteLine("    white-Space: nowrap;")
txtstream.WriteLine(" Next")
txtstream.WriteLine(".th")
txtstream.WriteLine("")
txtstream.WriteLine("    BORDER-RIGHT: #999999 2px solid;")
txtstream.WriteLine("    PADDING-RIGHT: 6px;")
txtstream.WriteLine("    PADDING-LEFT: 6px;")
txtstream.WriteLine("    FONT-WEIGHT: Bold;")
txtstream.WriteLine("    PADDING-BOTTOM: 6px;")
txtstream.WriteLine("    COLOR: black;")
txtstream.WriteLine("    PADDING-TOP: 6px;")
txtstream.WriteLine("    BORDER-BOTTOM: #999 2px solid;")
txtstream.WriteLine("    BACKGROUND-COLOR: #eeeeee;")
txtstream.WriteLine("    FONT-FAMILY: font-family: Cambria, serif;")
txtstream.WriteLine("    FONT-SIZE: 10px;")
txtstream.WriteLine("    text-align: right;")
txtstream.WriteLine("    white-Space: nowrap;")
txtstream.WriteLine(" Next")
txtstream.WriteLine("td")
txtstream.WriteLine("")
txtstream.WriteLine("    BORDER-RIGHT: #999999 3px solid;")
txtstream.WriteLine("    PADDING-RIGHT: 6px;")
txtstream.WriteLine("    PADDING-LEFT: 6px;")
txtstream.WriteLine("    FONT-WEIGHT: Normal;")
txtstream.WriteLine("    PADDING-BOTTOM: 6px;")
txtstream.WriteLine("    COLOR: navy;")
txtstream.WriteLine("    LINE-HEIGHT: 14px;")
txtstream.WriteLine("    PADDING-TOP: 6px;")
txtstream.WriteLine("    BORDER-BOTTOM: #999 1px solid;")
txtstream.WriteLine("    BACKGROUND-COLOR: #eeeeee;")
```

```
txtstream.WriteLine("    FONT-FAMILY: font-family: Cambria, serif;")
txtstream.WriteLine("    FONT-SIZE: 12px;")
txtstream.WriteLine("    text-align: left;")
txtstream.WriteLine("    white-Space: nowrap;")
txtstream.WriteLine(" Next")
txtstream.WriteLine("div")
txtstream.WriteLine("")
txtstream.WriteLine("    BORDER-RIGHT: #999999 3px solid;")
txtstream.WriteLine("    PADDING-RIGHT: 6px;")
txtstream.WriteLine("    PADDING-LEFT: 6px;")
txtstream.WriteLine("    FONT-WEIGHT: Normal;")
txtstream.WriteLine("    PADDING-BOTTOM: 6px;")
txtstream.WriteLine("    COLOR: white;")
txtstream.WriteLine("    PADDING-TOP: 6px;")
txtstream.WriteLine("    BORDER-BOTTOM: #999 1px solid;")
txtstream.WriteLine("    BACKGROUND-COLOR: navy;")
txtstream.WriteLine("    FONT-FAMILY: font-family: Cambria, serif;")
txtstream.WriteLine("    FONT-SIZE: 10px;")
txtstream.WriteLine("    text-align: left;")
txtstream.WriteLine("    white-Space: nowrap;")
txtstream.WriteLine(" Next")
txtstream.WriteLine("span")
txtstream.WriteLine("")
txtstream.WriteLine("    BORDER-RIGHT: #999999 3px solid;")
txtstream.WriteLine("    PADDING-RIGHT: 3px;")
txtstream.WriteLine("    PADDING-LEFT: 3px;")
txtstream.WriteLine("    FONT-WEIGHT: Normal;")
txtstream.WriteLine("    PADDING-BOTTOM: 3px;")
txtstream.WriteLine("    COLOR: white;")
txtstream.WriteLine("    PADDING-TOP: 3px;")
txtstream.WriteLine("    BORDER-BOTTOM: #999 1px solid;")
txtstream.WriteLine("    BACKGROUND-COLOR: navy;")
txtstream.WriteLine("    FONT-FAMILY: font-family: Cambria, serif;")
```

```
txtstream.WriteLine("    FONT-SIZE: 10px;")
txtstream.WriteLine("    text-align: left;")
txtstream.WriteLine("    white-Space: nowrap;")
txtstream.WriteLine("    display:inline-block;")
txtstream.WriteLine("    width: 100%;")
txtstream.WriteLine(" Next")
txtstream.WriteLine("textarea")
txtstream.WriteLine("")
txtstream.WriteLine("    BORDER-RIGHT: #999999 3px solid;")
txtstream.WriteLine("    PADDING-RIGHT: 3px;")
txtstream.WriteLine("    PADDING-LEFT: 3px;")
txtstream.WriteLine("    FONT-WEIGHT: Normal;")
txtstream.WriteLine("    PADDING-BOTTOM: 3px;")
txtstream.WriteLine("    COLOR: white;")
txtstream.WriteLine("    PADDING-TOP: 3px;")
txtstream.WriteLine("    BORDER-BOTTOM: #999 1px solid;")
txtstream.WriteLine("    BACKGROUND-COLOR: navy;")
txtstream.WriteLine("    FONT-FAMILY: font-family: Cambria, serif;")
txtstream.WriteLine("    FONT-SIZE: 10px;")
txtstream.WriteLine("    text-align: left;")
txtstream.WriteLine("    white-Space: nowrap;")
txtstream.WriteLine("    width: 100%;")
txtstream.WriteLine(" Next")
txtstream.WriteLine("select")
txtstream.WriteLine("")
txtstream.WriteLine("    BORDER-RIGHT: #999999 3px solid;")
txtstream.WriteLine("    PADDING-RIGHT: 6px;")
txtstream.WriteLine("    PADDING-LEFT: 6px;")
txtstream.WriteLine("    FONT-WEIGHT: Normal;")
txtstream.WriteLine("    PADDING-BOTTOM: 6px;")
txtstream.WriteLine("    COLOR: white;")
txtstream.WriteLine("    PADDING-TOP: 6px;")
txtstream.WriteLine("    BORDER-BOTTOM: #999 1px solid;")
```

```
txtstream.WriteLine("   BACKGROUND-COLOR: navy;")
txtstream.WriteLine("   FONT-FAMILY: font-family: Cambria, serif;")
txtstream.WriteLine("   FONT-SIZE: 10px;")
txtstream.WriteLine("   text-align: left;")
txtstream.WriteLine("   white-Space: nowrap;")
txtstream.WriteLine("   width: 100%;")
txtstream.WriteLine(" Next")
txtstream.WriteLine("input")
txtstream.WriteLine(""")
txtstream.WriteLine("   BORDER-RIGHT: #999999 3px solid;")
txtstream.WriteLine("   PADDING-RIGHT: 3px;")
txtstream.WriteLine("   PADDING-LEFT: 3px;")
txtstream.WriteLine("   FONT-WEIGHT: Bold;")
txtstream.WriteLine("   PADDING-BOTTOM: 3px;")
txtstream.WriteLine("   COLOR: white;")
txtstream.WriteLine("   PADDING-TOP: 3px;")
txtstream.WriteLine("   BORDER-BOTTOM: #999 1px solid;")
txtstream.WriteLine("   BACKGROUND-COLOR: navy;")
txtstream.WriteLine("   FONT-FAMILY: font-family: Cambria, serif;")
txtstream.WriteLine("   FONT-SIZE: 12px;")
txtstream.WriteLine("   text-align: left;")
txtstream.WriteLine("   display:table-cell;")
txtstream.WriteLine("   white-Space: nowrap;")
txtstream.WriteLine("   width: 100%;")
txtstream.WriteLine(" Next")
txtstream.WriteLine("h1 ")
txtstream.WriteLine("color: antiquewhite;")
txtstream.WriteLine("text-shadow: 1px 1px 1px black;")
txtstream.WriteLine("padding: 3px;")
txtstream.WriteLine("text-align: center;")
txtstream.WriteLine("box-shadow: inSet 2px 2px 5px rgba(0,0,0,0.5), inSet -
2px -2px 5px rgba(255,255,255,0.5);")
txtstream.WriteLine(" Next")
```

txtstream.WriteLine("</style>")

SHADOW BOX

txtstream.WriteLine("<style type='text/css'>")
txtstream.WriteLine("body")
txtstream.WriteLine("")
txtstream.WriteLine("   PADDING-RIGHT: 0px;")
txtstream.WriteLine("   PADDING-LEFT: 0px;")
txtstream.WriteLine("   PADDING-BOTTOM: 0px;")
txtstream.WriteLine("   MARGIN: 0px;")
txtstream.WriteLine("   COLOR: #333;")
txtstream.WriteLine("   PADDING-TOP: 0px;")
txtstream.WriteLine("   FONT-FAMILY: verdana, arial, helvetica, sans-serif;")
txtstream.WriteLine(" Next")
txtstream.WriteLine("table")
txtstream.WriteLine("")
txtstream.WriteLine("   BORDER-RIGHT: #999999 1px solid;")
txtstream.WriteLine("   PADDING-RIGHT: 1px;")
txtstream.WriteLine("   PADDING-LEFT: 1px;")
txtstream.WriteLine("   PADDING-BOTTOM: 1px;")
txtstream.WriteLine("   LINE-HEIGHT: 8px;")
txtstream.WriteLine("   PADDING-TOP: 1px;")
txtstream.WriteLine("   BORDER-BOTTOM: #999 1px solid;")
txtstream.WriteLine("   BACKGROUND-COLOR: #eeeeee;")
txtstream.WriteLine("
filter:progid:DXImageTransform.Microsoft.Shadow(color='silver',   Direction=135,
Strength=16)")
txtstream.WriteLine(" Next")
txtstream.WriteLine("th")
txtstream.WriteLine("")
txtstream.WriteLine("   BORDER-RIGHT: #999999 3px solid;")
txtstream.WriteLine("   PADDING-RIGHT: 6px;")

```
txtstream.WriteLine("   PADDING-LEFT: 6px;")
txtstream.WriteLine("   FONT-WEIGHT: Bold;")
txtstream.WriteLine("   FONT-SIZE: 14px;")
txtstream.WriteLine("   PADDING-BOTTOM: 6px;")
txtstream.WriteLine("   COLOR: darkred;")
txtstream.WriteLine("   LINE-HEIGHT: 14px;")
txtstream.WriteLine("   PADDING-TOP: 6px;")
txtstream.WriteLine("   BORDER-BOTTOM: #999 1px solid;")
txtstream.WriteLine("   BACKGROUND-COLOR: #eeeeee;")
txtstream.WriteLine("   FONT-FAMILY: font-family: Cambria, serif;")
txtstream.WriteLine("   FONT-SIZE: 12px;")
txtstream.WriteLine("   text-align: left;")
txtstream.WriteLine("   white-Space: nowrap;")
txtstream.WriteLine(" Next")
txtstream.WriteLine(".th")
txtstream.WriteLine("“)
txtstream.WriteLine("   BORDER-RIGHT: #999999 2px solid;")
txtstream.WriteLine("   PADDING-RIGHT: 6px;")
txtstream.WriteLine("   PADDING-LEFT: 6px;")
txtstream.WriteLine("   FONT-WEIGHT: Bold;")
txtstream.WriteLine("   PADDING-BOTTOM: 6px;")
txtstream.WriteLine("   COLOR: black;")
txtstream.WriteLine("   PADDING-TOP: 6px;")
txtstream.WriteLine("   BORDER-BOTTOM: #999 2px solid;")
txtstream.WriteLine("   BACKGROUND-COLOR: #eeeeee;")
txtstream.WriteLine("   FONT-FAMILY: font-family: Cambria, serif;")
txtstream.WriteLine("   FONT-SIZE: 10px;")
txtstream.WriteLine("   text-align: right;")
txtstream.WriteLine("   white-Space: nowrap;")
txtstream.WriteLine(" Next")
txtstream.WriteLine("td")
txtstream.WriteLine("“)
txtstream.WriteLine("   BORDER-RIGHT: #999999 3px solid;")
```

```
txtstream.WriteLine("    PADDING-RIGHT: 6px;")
txtstream.WriteLine("    PADDING-LEFT: 6px;")
txtstream.WriteLine("    FONT-WEIGHT: Normal;")
txtstream.WriteLine("    PADDING-BOTTOM: 6px;")
txtstream.WriteLine("    COLOR: navy;")
txtstream.WriteLine("    LINE-HEIGHT: 14px;")
txtstream.WriteLine("    PADDING-TOP: 6px;")
txtstream.WriteLine("    BORDER-BOTTOM: #999 1px solid;")
txtstream.WriteLine("    BACKGROUND-COLOR: #eeeeee;")
txtstream.WriteLine("    FONT-FAMILY: font-family: Cambria, serif;")
txtstream.WriteLine("    FONT-SIZE: 12px;")
txtstream.WriteLine("    text-align: left;")
txtstream.WriteLine("    white-Space: nowrap;")
txtstream.WriteLine(" Next")
txtstream.WriteLine("div")
txtstream.WriteLine("")
txtstream.WriteLine("    BORDER-RIGHT: #999999 3px solid;")
txtstream.WriteLine("    PADDING-RIGHT: 6px;")
txtstream.WriteLine("    PADDING-LEFT: 6px;")
txtstream.WriteLine("    FONT-WEIGHT: Normal;")
txtstream.WriteLine("    PADDING-BOTTOM: 6px;")
txtstream.WriteLine("    COLOR: white;")
txtstream.WriteLine("    PADDING-TOP: 6px;")
txtstream.WriteLine("    BORDER-BOTTOM: #999 1px solid;")
txtstream.WriteLine("    BACKGROUND-COLOR: navy;")
txtstream.WriteLine("    FONT-FAMILY: font-family: Cambria, serif;")
txtstream.WriteLine("    FONT-SIZE: 10px;")
txtstream.WriteLine("    text-align: left;")
txtstream.WriteLine("    white-Space: nowrap;")
txtstream.WriteLine(" Next")
txtstream.WriteLine("span")
txtstream.WriteLine("")
txtstream.WriteLine("    BORDER-RIGHT: #999999 3px solid;")
```

```
txtstream.WriteLine("    PADDING-RIGHT: 3px;")
txtstream.WriteLine("    PADDING-LEFT: 3px;")
txtstream.WriteLine("    FONT-WEIGHT: Normal;")
txtstream.WriteLine("    PADDING-BOTTOM: 3px;")
txtstream.WriteLine("    COLOR: white;")
txtstream.WriteLine("    PADDING-TOP: 3px;")
txtstream.WriteLine("    BORDER-BOTTOM: #999 1px solid;")
txtstream.WriteLine("    BACKGROUND-COLOR: navy;")
txtstream.WriteLine("    FONT-FAMILY: font-family: Cambria, serif;")
txtstream.WriteLine("    FONT-SIZE: 10px;")
txtstream.WriteLine("    text-align: left;")
txtstream.WriteLine("    white-Space: nowrap;")
txtstream.WriteLine("    display: inline-block;")
txtstream.WriteLine("    width: 100%;")
txtstream.WriteLine(" Next")
txtstream.WriteLine("textarea")
txtstream.WriteLine("")
txtstream.WriteLine("    BORDER-RIGHT: #999999 3px solid;")
txtstream.WriteLine("    PADDING-RIGHT: 3px;")
txtstream.WriteLine("    PADDING-LEFT: 3px;")
txtstream.WriteLine("    FONT-WEIGHT: Normal;")
txtstream.WriteLine("    PADDING-BOTTOM: 3px;")
txtstream.WriteLine("    COLOR: white;")
txtstream.WriteLine("    PADDING-TOP: 3px;")
txtstream.WriteLine("    BORDER-BOTTOM: #999 1px solid;")
txtstream.WriteLine("    BACKGROUND-COLOR: navy;")
txtstream.WriteLine("    FONT-FAMILY: font-family: Cambria, serif;")
txtstream.WriteLine("    FONT-SIZE: 10px;")
txtstream.WriteLine("    text-align: left;")
txtstream.WriteLine("    white-Space: nowrap;")
txtstream.WriteLine("    width: 100%;")
txtstream.WriteLine(" Next")
txtstream.WriteLine("select")
```

```
txtstream.WriteLine("")
txtstream.WriteLine("   BORDER-RIGHT: #999999 3px solid;")
txtstream.WriteLine("   PADDING-RIGHT: 6px;")
txtstream.WriteLine("   PADDING-LEFT: 6px;")
txtstream.WriteLine("   FONT-WEIGHT: Normal;")
txtstream.WriteLine("   PADDING-BOTTOM: 6px;")
txtstream.WriteLine("   COLOR: white;")
txtstream.WriteLine("   PADDING-TOP: 6px;")
txtstream.WriteLine("   BORDER-BOTTOM: #999 1px solid;")
txtstream.WriteLine("   BACKGROUND-COLOR: navy;")
txtstream.WriteLine("   FONT-FAMILY: font-family: Cambria, serif;")
txtstream.WriteLine("   FONT-SIZE: 10px;")
txtstream.WriteLine("   text-align: left;")
txtstream.WriteLine("   white-Space: nowrap;")
txtstream.WriteLine("   width: 100%;")
txtstream.WriteLine(" Next")
txtstream.WriteLine("input")
txtstream.WriteLine("")
txtstream.WriteLine("   BORDER-RIGHT: #999999 3px solid;")
txtstream.WriteLine("   PADDING-RIGHT: 3px;")
txtstream.WriteLine("   PADDING-LEFT: 3px;")
txtstream.WriteLine("   FONT-WEIGHT: Bold;")
txtstream.WriteLine("   PADDING-BOTTOM: 3px;")
txtstream.WriteLine("   COLOR: white;")
txtstream.WriteLine("   PADDING-TOP: 3px;")
txtstream.WriteLine("   BORDER-BOTTOM: #999 1px solid;")
txtstream.WriteLine("   BACKGROUND-COLOR: navy;")
txtstream.WriteLine("   FONT-FAMILY: font-family: Cambria, serif;")
txtstream.WriteLine("   FONT-SIZE: 12px;")
txtstream.WriteLine("   text-align: left;")
txtstream.WriteLine("   display: table-cell;")
txtstream.WriteLine("   white-Space: nowrap;")
txtstream.WriteLine("   width: 100%;")
```

```
txtstream.WriteLine(" Next")
txtstream.WriteLine("h1 ")
txtstream.WriteLine("color: antiquewhite;")
txtstream.WriteLine("text-shadow: 1px 1px 1px black;")
txtstream.WriteLine("padding: 3px;")
txtstream.WriteLine("text-align: center;")
txtstream.WriteLine("box-shadow: inSet 2px 2px 5px rgba(0,0,0,0.5), inSet -2px -2px 5px rgba(255,255,255,0.5);")
txtstream.WriteLine(" Next")
txtstream.WriteLine("</style>")
```

www.ingramcontent.com/pod-product-compliance
Lightning Source LLC
Chambersburg PA
CBHW070843070326
40690CB00009B/1670